Overwhelmed
& Grateful

Books by Jillian Benfield

The Gift of the Unexpected
Overwhelmed & Grateful

Overwhelmed & Grateful

The Key to Finding God's Goodness in All Life's Ups & Downs

JILLIAN BENFIELD

BETHANY HOUSE

a division of Baker Publishing Group

Minneapolis, Minnesota

© 2025 by Jillian Lee Benfield

Published by Bethany House Publishers
Minneapolis, Minnesota
BethanyHouse.com

Bethany House Publishers is a division of
Baker Publishing Group, Grand Rapids, Michigan

Library of Congress Cataloging-in-Publication Data
Names: Benfield, Jillian, author
Title: Overwhelmed & grateful : the key to finding God's goodness in all life's
   ups and downs / Jillian Benfield.
Other titles: Overwhelmed and grateful
Description: Minneapolis, Minnesota : Bethany House Publishers, a division of
   Baker Publishing Group, [2025] | Includes bibliographical references.
Identifiers: LCCN 2025001603 | ISBN 9780764244124 (paperback) | ISBN
   9780764244940 (casebound) | ISBN 9781493450718 (ebook)
Subjects: LCSH: Resilience (Personality trait)—Religious Aspects—Christianity |
   Hope—Religious aspects—Christianity | Christian women—Religious life
Classification: LCC BV4597.58.R47 B46 2025 | DDC 234/.25—dc23/
   eng/20250326
LC record available at https://lccn.loc.gov/2025001603

Cover design by Micah Kandros Design

The author is represented by the literary agency of Mary DeMuth Literary.

Baker Publishing Group publications use paper produced from sustainable forestry practices and postconsumer waste whenever possible.

25 26 27 28 29 30 31   7 6 5 4 3 2 1

For my mom, Joanne,
who has held me through the storms
& by her presence, helped me point
my face toward the sun.
Thank you, Suzy Sunshine.

Contents

Part 3 REORDER

Foreword

YEARS AGO, a dear friend of mine received a life-changing diagnosis.

Breast cancer.

Hearing the word *cancer* at any age is devastating, of course. But she was only in her early thirties.

Young. Healthy. A wife and mom of three little boys.

I couldn't comprehend it. I know she felt the same.

I had many conversations with God about this one. We talk often, though I tend to do most of the talking.

"God, why does she have cancer? I don't understand. Help me understand."

During one particularly hard day of motherhood, I was venting to this friend about something going on in my life. I can't remember what it was—probably exhaustion and overwhelm from parenting my own small kids.

After a few minutes of talking, I realized I had been going on and on about my situation, which made me feel insensitive to my friend.

Her problems, of course, seemed so much bigger in my mind. Sure, I had stress—don't we all? But I didn't have cancer. What did I have to complain about?

"I'm so sorry," I told her. "This must seem small and petty to you. I should stop complaining—this is nothing compared to what you're going through."

I'll never forget her response.

"Leslie, just because my version of hard is different than yours doesn't make it any less hard. What you're going through is a lot for you. Don't compare the two. I'm here for you, just as you're here for me."

Mic. Drop.

Just because my version of hard is different from yours doesn't make it any less valid.

Her beautiful words helped me embrace my own struggles and gave me empathy for the hardships of others. I watched this woman undergo rounds of medical treatments to save her life, all while radiating love and gratitude.

She often showed up to chemo in her wedding gown, determined to find joy even as life-saving poison coursed through her veins.

She shared her story with strangers online.

She smiled and cried and wasn't afraid to tell the world that what she was going through was pretty dang hard.

She was in the muck and still found joy and—*gasp*—had enough energy to sit with others facing their own battles.

She is my hero. I'm not sure she realizes how much her strength, compassion, and love for life changed me.

And by the grace of God, she has been cancer-free for years.

My friend reminded me we each face our own version of hard. But life is too short to simply wish it away. I'm old enough now to know that saying things like, "Hey, God, if you can just get me through this week, then I'm sure I'll be able to relax," is laughable.

Ha! Remember the old saying? If you want to hear God laugh, tell Him your plans.

The reality is, we're all going to face challenges along this journey. And just when we get through one, *BAM*—another one takes its place.

What gets us through is finding joy in the midst of it and making space to empathize with others—even when their struggles don't look like ours.

That's what gives us hope.

Love.

Compassion.

Empathy.

Wisdom.

That's what makes us better humans.

Just because I'm going through my own version of hard doesn't make yours any less real. I'm here for you.

And do you know who else embodies this truth so well? Jillian.

She knows that not all women will walk her exact journey. But because of it, she's able to sit with others—either in person or metaphorically, through this beautiful book—to help us all see through the hard and find goodness within it.

This book is a gift. Not just because it's filled with Jillian's inspiring words, but because, as she so beautifully states:

There is no line dividing the secular and the sacred. God's fingerprints mark it all. Our job is to recognize it. To recognize this Love who is ever-present in us and in each other, in nature and in the good things God inspired people to create.

I want to create pause, to sit in awe, to thank God for life's beauty in busy times, in times of heartbreak and when I am finding my way to new ground.

Same, Jillian. Same.

Dear reader, what you're going through is hard.

But there's hope in the darkness. There's joy in the hurt. There's love in the pain.

Let's figure this out together.

—Leslie Means, founder of Her View From Home
and author of *So God Made a Mother*
and *So God Made a Grandma*

Introduction

Here is the world. Beautiful and terrible things will happen.
Don't be afraid.

—Frederick Buechner, *Beyond Words:*
Daily Readings in the ABC's of Faith

YEARS AGO, I had one of the saddest conversations of my
life. The conversation wasn't about death; it wasn't about
grief. It was about beauty.

It was late September 2016 when my husband, Andy, and
I, with our three-year-old and eighteen-month-old, boarded
a plane in Tucson, Arizona, caught another in Las Vegas, and
landed in Atlanta to join Andy's family in putting his grand-
father, Fred Sr., to rest. We drove through Atlanta traffic to
the North Georgia funeral home where Fred, a World War
II veteran, husband, and father of five, lay.

We arrived at the Georgia funeral home with our toddlers
in tow. We saw Grandpa from afar. We made small talk with
distant relatives while the smell of disinfectant, lilies, and
embalming chemicals hung in the air. A deacon arrived and

asked if anyone wanted to share something about Fred Sr., and many did.

But that's not where the sad conversation took place.

It unfolded afterward at my in-laws' house. Family from Georgia and the Midwest sat where they could find a chair or an open spot on the couch. The house was filled with an array of covered dishes brought in by neighbors and loved ones. There were paper plates to serve yourself. There was chatter, lots of it. In other words, there was life. There was death and there was life. Life among the death.

I sat across from the eldest people at the gathering at the black and cherry kitchen table. They were distant relatives I had never met. We talked about another relative who couldn't make it to the funeral. This relative lived in one of the most beautiful places in the United States. The old woman sitting across from me told me how harsh and how very long the winters could be there.

I asked her, "Do the mountains and lakes make up for it a bit?"

She replied, "Oh, it all just becomes the background."[1]

Just the background—how sad, I thought.

We were a military family at the time and moved more than the average military family. As someone who had spent only three years living amid the Nevada, New Mexico, and Arizona mountains, I couldn't fathom their beauty fading into the background. The mountains were alive to me, a part of my every day. They were a constant. They sustained me through many hard years, years I will tell you about later in this book. They were a reminder that God's beauty, God's goodness, God's self are here, right here. *Even* here. *Even now.*

I forgot about the exchange until years later. After spending three years in mountainless Texas, the military assigned us to Colorado—our dream location. A location I thought we would never leave. Life leveled out there. After many tumultuous years for our family, we had finally made it to our desired destination: one with fewer medical appointments and medical scares, with more resources and less anxiety over school systems for our son with a disability. And we were back in the mountains.

Then, one day, I drove from our home to drop off my youngest at preschool. At the top of the hill, before the turn into the church parking lot, was the most spectacular panoramic view of the entire Colorado Springs mountain range, surrounding its crown jewel—Pike's Peak. Normally, the view made me gasp, or had me praying a simple two-word prayer, *Thank you*. But on that day, I had no reaction.

The beauty had become the background.

It was a wake-up call, a warning sign that something was off.

Life can be overwhelming even when it's steady. This book is called *Overwhelmed & Grateful*. You'll encounter that overwhelm in each of the chapters ahead. Overwhelm looks like anger and confusion. Overwhelm looks like longing and tears. Even if we are not in a place of overwhelming busyness or grief, even when we are not experiencing a life change that has us reeling, there's so often something or someone who needs more of us—more of us than we sometimes feel capable of giving. We are pulled in multiple directions at once when life has been turned upside down and even when it is right side up.

When things are steady, there are still schedules to manage, deadlines to meet, and laundry always in need of folding. All while trying to fit in exercising, getting enough sleep, and drinking enough water too! And it is so often overwhelming. When our calendars, our minds, and our hearts are brimming, it's easy to miss the beauty all around us. When our children's giggles don't make us pause and breathe in thanks, when our spouse touches the small of our back and we can't feel that quick burst of love, or when we can't see the presence of the Divine in the nearby wheat field, the swaying palm trees, or the mountains, it's time to create pause. It's time to start paying attention to the beauty once more.

There is no line dividing the secular and the sacred. God's fingerprints mark it all. Our job is to recognize it. To recognize this Love who is ever-present in us and in each other, in nature and in the good things God inspired people to create.

I want to create pause, to sit in awe, to thank God for life's beauty in busy times, in times of heartbreak, and when I am finding my way to new ground. I believe it was my time in those upside-down years that taught me to look for beauty. I was desperate to find something good to hold on to. Now that life has settled, now that my want has lessened, I have found that keeping an eye out for beauty requires daily practice. I have found that I cannot always fix overwhelm and yet I can look for beauty within it. I am hoping you will join me in searching.

Because I do not want to become an old woman who let the beauty of her life become the background. I have a feeling you don't want to become an old woman who missed the good and lovely things of your one precious life either.

But what does the spiritual practice of recognizing and being thankful for beauty look like when life is really hard? What does it look like when you are covered in baby spit-up and taking a conference call in your unkempt house? What does it look like when the unexpected has upended your life—instead of walking your neighborhood each morning you are now walking the hospital hallways, praying for rescue? What does it look like after one of life's metaphorical storms has passed, but the storm blew you off course and you are living in a place that feels unrecognizable?

Western culture often tells us we should downplay the hard parts of our lives and just focus on the positive.

"Look on the bright side!"

"It could be worse!"

"Good vibes only!"

These sayings and others ring in our conversations and echo in our minds when hard times hit. Yet, forced positivity can be dangerous. Toxic positivity "is defined as the act of rejecting or denying stress, negativity, or other negative experiences that exist."[2]

Multiple studies have found that denying our emotions makes us depressed and physically ill.[3] A Harvard study found that people who bottle up their emotions even increase their chance of premature death from all causes by more than 30 percent, with their risk of being diagnosed with cancer increasing by 70 percent.[4] As author and researcher Dr. Brené Brown puts it, when we deny emotions, they own us.[5]

Research points us to be more candid, more honest about our emotions instead of ignoring them. However, research also consistently shows that practicing gratitude leads to a happier life.

The word *gratitude* comes from "the Latin word *gratia*, which means grace, graciousness, or gratefulness."[6] According to researchers at Harvard Medical School, in the process of practicing gratitude, people usually recognize that the source of goodness in their lives "lies at least partially outside themselves," and consequently, being grateful also helps us connect to something larger than ourselves.[7]

In the past two decades, social scientists have found gratitude to have measurable benefits for nearly every area of our lives.[8] The Greater Good Science Center at the University of California, Berkeley describes gratitude as the "social glue" that inspires people to be more generous, kind, and helpful and key to building and nurturing strong relationships.[9]

So, what is gratitude? Gratitude is the act of recognizing and being thankful for goodness and beauty. Gratitude is a feeling we get when we acknowledge this goodness, and it is more than a feeling.

Diana Butler Bass, the author of *Grateful*, writes that gratitude is also an awareness.

> Gratitude is not only the emotional response to random experiences, but even in the darkest times of life, gratitude waits to be seen, recognized and acted upon more thoughtfully and with a sense of purpose. Gratitude is a feeling, but it is also more than that. And it is much more than a spiritual technique to achieve peace of mind or prosperity. Gratitude is a habit of awareness that reshapes our self-understanding and the moral choices we make in the world.[10]

Gratitude requires a heightened awareness. This noticing can sustain us and it has the power to change us. Gratitude is required to transform into the people we are meant to become.

I believe that gratitude helps us to connect to the source of life itself, and when we are more in touch with our Creator, we begin to live out the full life God dreams for us—one marked by love.

There is a paradox here:

Denying our emotions harms us.

Practicing gratitude—a habit that requires us to look at the good and positive aspects of life—helps us.

So how do we deal with these two seemingly competing truths?

How do we recognize beauty and be thankful for it at the graveside?

How do we practice gratitude when someone who promised to love us forever leaves?

How do we move forward when we are carrying a tormented past we wish we could trade?

The word *and*, or *&*.

———— & ————

The history of the ampersand is rooted in ancient Rome. The exact date of its creation is unknown, but the first record of *&* was found beneath the ash of the volcanic eruption that buried Pompeii in 79 AD. The writer was linking the letters *e* and *t*—forming the word *et* in Latin, which translates to the word *and* in English.[11] The ampersand is a link, a connection.

My history with the ampersand began in 2017—the year I gave birth to my youngest son, Preston, in Texas. Preston was diagnosed with posterior urethral valves in utero. I will tell more of his story later, but just know that the year he was born was one of the most difficult years of my life. Between Preston and my son Anderson, who has Down syndrome, the boys had eighteen specialists between them, my husband tells me. I add this detail of my husband recounting this because every day I was simply surviving and trying to make sure my boys more than survived.

That year, I read a Facebook post by Rachel Whalen about how the word *and* helps us to live more truthfully.[12] I could feel scared and worn out from my child's medical conditions *&* I could feel incredibly grateful that the worst—the worst that we were told in an ultrasound at fourteen weeks gestation—had not come to pass.

Before reading that article, I may have described this time in my life like this: "This is the hardest my life has ever been *but* I'm so grateful my sons are here and their medical conditions are improving!"

We are conditioned to frame things this way—in the *but* of things. We are conditioned to shine a light on the positive, otherwise we fear we are just sad, negative people.

However, unlike the word *and* that connects two ideas, the word *but* often does the opposite. *But* disconnects a statement that has already been made. When we use *but*, we negate the first part of our truth. Or, at the very least, downplay it. One of my main objectives with this book is for us to become *&* users. Because *&* helps us live in the fullness of our realities; *&* is our reminder that two competing emotions can be true at once. We can honor the darker parts of our reality while also practicing gratitude—the act of looking for and being thankful for the goodness around us and in us. Because God's goodness is always at work.

Gratitude is not the act of denying our hard circumstances; instead, it looks for beauty wherever our feet take us. In the mundane, in the sorrow, and in the rebuilding, the Divine is there—whispering the ways of love. Gratitude, in many ways, is the act of paying attention to this love that is always beating.

I wrote in my first book, *The Gift of the Unexpected*, that the closest I ever felt to God's presence was in the fifth-floor waiting room of a hospital while my son was undergoing open-heart surgery. I could tell you that day was awful and it would be true *&* I can tell you that I experienced peace like never before. That would also be true. With *&*, we don't have to choose. Gratitude is not a cure *&* gratitude can play a part in our healing when no cure is available. We have permission to live into our beautiful *&* difficult realities. We can be honest about what hurts, confuses, or even angers us & we can be on the lookout for God's beauty still unfolding. & is the spiritual practice of noticing. & is a prayer.

In his book *The Spirituality of the Psalms*, Old Testament scholar Walter Brueggemann divides the Psalms into three categories:

- Psalms of Orientation reflect the goodness of God's creation and order.
- Psalms of Disorientation reflect our periods of hurt, anguish, and confusion.
- Psalms of New Orientation reflect when joy breaks through once more and the psalmist is overwhelmed with gratitude for the new gifts God has given.[13]

Brueggemann writes, "The flow of human life characteristically is located either in the actual experience of one of these settings or is in movement from one to another."[14]

In this book, we will call the rhythms of life Order, Disorder, and Reorder.

- **Order**—when life is relatively steady, even a bit predictable, and we can live at a day-to-day pace. Of course, even when our feet find a solid path, there is inevitably a bump along the way that makes us trip. No pathway exists without an ill-placed stone or a twisty root that can make us lose our balance. Or perhaps you're walking with a heavier backpack than most. You carry this added challenge or pain with you, yet you've learned how to manage. You know how to move through life with it, even if at times it feels like too much. Being in a place of Order doesn't mean life is without hardships, but for the most part, these challenges are an expected disruption, since we know life is never perfect.

- **Disorder**—when an unexpected storm has come into our lives. We move to this place often by surprise, and the surprise is not a welcome one. Even if we know an ending is on the horizon, nothing can fully prepare us for the storm's level of impact. The tempest blows trees down onto the path we once knew. Our feet are no longer touching the ground. The terrain, our lives, are now unrecognizable, and it is devastating. We must make our way through the debris to find a new path.

- **Reorder**—when we have made our way through the wreckage of the storm. We find ourselves on that familiar path but it is not quite the same as we remember. Traces of the storm still linger & there are new things along the path because of the storm. The storm cleared shrubs and made way for new life to bloom. We are surprised by God's love breaking through once more. We are amazed by how we have changed through it too.

Brueggemann insists his Orientation, Disorientation, and New Orientation method is not meant to be a straitjacket.[15] We will take the same approach in this book. I believe we can experience a sense of Order in a Disordered period and Disorder once we have found our way to Reorder. Life is complex. I use these categories so we can discover how to practice the *& life* in all its ups and downs. It is also why you will see a suggested reading of a Psalm at the end of each chapter. The Psalms speak to us because they reflect the lives we have—lives that are so very often overwhelming. This overwhelming life is filled with great suffering & great joys. Thank God, the Psalms teach us our humanity is allowed. More than half of the Psalms are laments. The Psalms show us how to be in relationship with our Creator in all of life's phases. The Psalms remind us that God is with us in the struggle & in the rebuilding. The Psalms are so often an act of &. They remind us that bad things happen and we are allowed to account the damage. The Psalms so often end in hope & end in trust that God sees us in our struggle and will somehow, some way, bring us to new life once more.

"Feeling is only half the equation," says Phillip Watkins, professor of psychology and author of *Gratitude and the Good Life*.[16] It is equally important to express gratitude to reap the benefits, according to Watkins.[17] That's why at the end of each chapter there is also a short "&" prompt, designed to get you to really think about hard realities you are facing or have faced and to reflect on where you can see beauty in these periods.

My hope is that when you close this book, you will find your own way of reflecting, meditating, or praying through the &'s in your life—whether in a journal, a note on your phone, or a pause in the middle of the day to acknowledge the harsh & be grateful for the lovely.

This is a book about gratitude and it is also about honesty. My hope is that this book, this practice of &, will help you become more honest than you ever have been. Honest with God, honest with the people in your life, and honest with yourself. Honesty takes in the whole picture. If you look at your life and only talk about the good, that's not being honest. If you look at your life and only see the bad, that's not honest either. Love is why you are here, and you cannot experience its fullness without honesty & gratitude. & can help you to go deeper than you have gone before in your relationships, in your endeavors, and in your faith. & can help you to live fully. This is what I hope for you. This is what I hope for myself—that we are fully alive while we are living.

Because when we are overwhelmed, we can get used to coasting. We can get used to living with grief and letting it be our only companion and not make room for anyone else to come in. We can get used to wanting to go back, back to better times, and forget to live the lives we have right now. We can get so used to the mountain view that instead of our appreciating its majesty, it becomes merely the background of our lives.

My hope for you when you close this book is that you will live into the &. Because to do so is to live into the life you actually have and into the life you are meant to co-create with the One who created you. & is honest. & is hopeful. & can remind you that even when the worst comes to pass, love still beats and love still creates. & love can help you live your life to the fullest and & can help you live into your fullest self—the version of you God dreamt up long ago.

I am writing this book from the vantage point of faith. Through years of enduring bad fundamentalist theology to years of agnosticism, I have arrived to this place where I believe Jesus was and is who He claimed to be. Even now, when the church disappoints me or confuses me or even has me wanting to run away—I can't get over Jesus. But you don't need to be a devoted Christian to join me on this journey of honoring the hard things & beautiful things of life. You just need to be open to this transformative process that can take place when we move from an either/or way of living and toward a both/and way of being.

In each chapter, we will explore the common emotions we experience at these different points of the human experience.

(And of course, we can feel all sorts of emotions no matter what rhythm of life we are in!) In each chapter, we will learn how to hold the dark in one hand, the light in the other, honoring both. This book will combine science, metaphor, and passages from the Bible to remind us of our humanity and to take refuge in the One who took on humanity.

Jesus entered the darkness with us, acknowledged its power, wept with us, was hungry and tired and misunderstood, like us. Jesus enjoyed friendships & ended up being betrayed by a friend. Jesus experienced the joy of healing people wherever He went & He experienced exhaustion. Jesus knew the deep trust of a friend that prompted him to walk on water & the same friend denied knowing Jesus in His darkest hour. Jesus knew the darkness & He was the light. He wants us to remember: Darkness is here & so too is the light. This light is more powerful than the darkness. This light is in us and all around us. This light is pointing out the good and pointing us toward a good life.

In this world, we will experience the full range of what it means to be human, and being human is so very hard. & we always have access to this light.

Let's learn to be the kind of people who have eyes to see, let's be the kind of people who create space to hold it all—the difficult & the beautiful.

Because life is both.

Let's be people who notice.

We get the beautiful life we are looking for when we acknowledge the darkness of this world & see God's love in all its forms whispering to us in the midst.

Beauty cannot fade to the background when we make a habit of whispering back, "Thank you."

REFLECTION QUESTIONS AS WE BEGIN

What rhythm of life are you in right now: Order, Disorder, or Reorder?

Is it easy or hard for you to see beauty right now? What is helping you or hindering you?

& REFLECTION

The overwhelm I am experiencing right now is:

& I can see beauty in my life right now in this way:

Part 1

ORDER

|||||||||||||||||||||||||||||

The movement of grace toward gratitude
brings us from the package of self-obsessed
madness to a spiritual awakening. Gratitude
is peace.

—Anne Lamott, *Help, Thanks, Wow:*
The Three Essential Prayers

1

Stressed & Grateful

I AM WRITING THIS BOOK from a place of Order. For five years, we lived in Disorder—where one unexpected thing hit after another, and where isolation, confusion, and depression were as thick as the Texas humidity we lived in during much of that time. Then came a beautiful era of Reorder, in which things settled and resettled, and we came out the other side of the storm, not unscathed, but changed and with a new perspective. I will go into more depth about this later because my story is not so different from yours. We have a shared humanity, and humanity comes with a constant interweaving of what is severe & what is good.

Now we are where I believe many of us spend most of our lives—in an Ordered place. It is that place where life is humming along, things are good, but good does not mean without struggle. Life is still life. We may be tempted to think that the mom with the well-dressed kids, or the guy who just got yet another promotion, or the ministry leader who seems to be so full of grace and whose words drip with a confusing amount of peace lack struggles. But they don't. That's not the world we live in. In other words, there's always something. There's always something beneath the surface of people's lives that they may not talk about. But it's there.

The American Psychological Association found in a 2014 study that the main sources of Americans' hardships were related to money, work, the economy, family responsibilities, and health.[1] Maybe that resonates with you. Or maybe it's a strained relationship, a rejection, a loss of purpose, a struggle with identity, a feeling of stuck-ness, an issue with a child, a struggle that is never far from your thoughts. These struggles can create stress.

The World Health Organization (WHO) defines stress as "a state of worry or mental tension caused by a difficult situation" and describes it as a "natural human response that prompts us to address challenges and threats in our lives."[2] WHO goes on to say that everyone experiences some degree of stress. Stress is not a disease but a response to an outside problem. It's how our bodies respond to tension physically, mentally, and emotionally.

When we face a threat, stress levels rise, and hormones such as cortisol are released to increase alertness. Stress can help us increase productivity when it comes in short bursts, but chronic stress can contribute to problems like high blood pressure, heart disease, and anxiety disorders.

We all have struggles that often create stress. This is not to say that all struggles are created equal—they're not. The struggles during an Ordered period are not the same struggles present in a Disordered phase—which may cause grief, trauma, or a dark night of the soul. However, at any point in our lives, there is likely something creating friction. Even when more than our basic needs are met, even when we have good support systems and healthy coping strategies, even when life is so very good, it can also be very challenging. & even when life is so very stressful, that does not erase the beauty that is still present.

---------- *&* ----------

FALL 2023
FLORIDA'S SPACE COAST

In 2023, I released my first book, and my husband became a partner in his orthodontic practice. It was the year our dreams finally came true. Then, the second half of 2023 came along. One of our children developed severe anxiety. This anxiety presented in both emotional and physical ways. We saw the light that normally shone so brightly within them start to fade.

It was sad, confusing, and scary for all of us. The fear of not knowing whether this type of anxiety was something they'd live with forever—along with guilt over the possibility that our tumultuous years might have affected them in ways that were hidden for a time and were only now beginning to reveal themselves—was incredibly stressful. The struggle intersected at the known we were greeted with daily and the unknown of what to do about it, and what might lie ahead.

This time didn't turn our lives upside down. It didn't end life as we knew it, as some of the events in our Disordered era had. Yet the stress was right there, bubbling right below the surface, never far from our thoughts.

My husband, Andy, and I almost canceled our long-awaited trip to Grand Teton and Yellowstone National Parks. Two years prior, when we were living in Colorado Springs, we had gotten news of a business opportunity for Andy in Florida. After years of our moving around with the military, Andy was getting out of the service, and we were permanently relocating to Florida—just forty-five minutes from where I grew up—to begin civilian life. I had Andy make me a promise: that we would continue to go back to the mountains after his orthodontic associateship was over. Because my soul feels at rest at the beach, like the one next to our home, but feels awake in the mountains. You never quite know what view is around the next corner of a hike or how the sun's position will highlight the mountain's peaks and crevices in ways you hadn't noticed the first time. The mountains are wild with God's beauty waiting to surprise us around each turn.

This was our first scheduled trip after Andy's associateship was complete and he became a partner in his practice. My mom convinced us nothing would change if we stayed home, and I knew she was right. So we went. God met us there. For five days we traded in salt air for the smell of fresh evergreens. We took one too many pictures of Jenny Lake and how it perfectly reflected the crisp blue sky above. We gasped as we made our way into Cascade Canyon, dotted with autumn-colored trees and plants that a mother and baby moose munched on for lunch. All while being enveloped by the silver, rocky points of the Tetons. For a day and a half, gratitude was easy to come by. We were so thankful for God's awe-inspiring beauty, we were so thankful for a support system that allowed us to experience it and connect in a way we needed after such a busy year. Gratitude poured out of our lips and our hearts. After thirty-six hours of being reacquainted with the beauty of the West, I called my mom when I knew the kids wouldn't be around, to get the real update. We were in our rental car making our way to

Yellowstone. It was very early, before the sun even thought about showing herself. We slowly made our way through Wyoming's wild landscape while getting the download of our hurting child's behavior from the past day and a half. I thought my parents being there might help ease their stress for a bit. I thought my dad's pillow fights, and the too many treats from my mom, would help lighten the load weighing on their minds. But it didn't. I hung up the phone and knew this was not a bump in the road but a new path we would be on for a while. I called a child psychologist and scheduled an appointment. Andy and I rode in near silence after that, each with a knot in the pit of our stomach. How were we supposed to stay here, in this place, so far away from home? How were we supposed to enjoy ourselves with these worries racing through our minds like the river flowing parallel to us as we made our way deeper into the park? We didn't say it to each other; we didn't have to. We knew we would have to push through the day, we would have to fight not to find beauty but to let it penetrate, to go past our eyes and into our beings.

Our first stop was Old Faithful. We had just missed an eruption. So we explored the Upper Geyser Basin just beyond the famed geyser. This area has the largest concentration of geysers and geothermal features in the world. One square mile contains at least 150 hydrothermal wonders. The heat for the hydrothermal features comes from Yellowstone's underground volcano. Rain and snow supply water that seeps several thousand feet below the surface where it is heated. Underground cracks form a natural plumbing system. Hot water rises through that system to produce hot springs and geysers.[3]

The world's most famous geyser, Old Faithful, may have us non-geologists thinking that geysers are predictable. We may assume we can set our watches and add or subtract ten minutes and then we will see their glory. However, it is impossible to predict the eruption time of most geysers because the complex interactions that take place beneath the surface are always changing. These include earthquakes and fluctuations in a system's water or heat supply. Most geysers share conduits with other hot springs or geysers. This means that a predictable geyser is separate, apart. Geysers like Old Faithful stand alone. Their predictability is an exception, not the standard. Most geysers are complex. Most geysers are wild.

Many of us were taught formulas as a way of experiencing the Divine. We were taught that morning and bedtime routines, weekly church attendance, and following the rules often set by men were the ways of experiencing God ourselves. In the effort to contain ourselves, to contain our behavior, we also tried to contain the One who created us. We called God's creation outside of mankind lesser—less worthy, less important. Some even demonized it at times, warning that seeing God within its beauty would be replacing God, would be worshiping the wrong thing. As author Brian McLaren puts it, "There is a bias against the earth because the gospel is presented as an evacuation plan."[4]

But what if the universe is not separate from God, but instead is an outpouring of Godself? How would our view of ourselves, of this world, change if we could learn to see God within every living thing, including us? How would the view we have of our struggles change if we dared to believe that deep beneath the surface, God is always at work, and that work ultimately is moving us toward something good?

Richard Rohr introduced me to an *incarnational worldview*, the view that God is in everything and everyone.[5] Anna Case-Winters, a professor of theology and author, offers us a metaphor to better grasp this idea. In this metaphor, God is the ocean, and the sponge is God's creation:

> If you could picture a sponge in the ocean, there's not a bit of it that isn't filled with the water of the ocean. And yet it, in itself, it's a finite thing. And the ocean is way bigger than the sponge. So, this way of talking about it, and of course it's all metaphor, I don't think there's an easy way to understand the mystery of the divine presence in all things, but this helps convey it because you get both the real presence, the intimacy of God's connection with the creation, and also the ultimacy of God as being beyond the creation itself.[6]

I believe this holy work of recognizing God in all things and yet God's being beyond all things, can help us recognize beauty and the goodness still present even in harsh circumstances. I believe this is a path forward to practicing gratitude. I believe this is how we live fully; this is how we become.

An incarnational worldview can help us see God not as some distant ruler we are merely meant to obey, but as a constant companion pulling us into communion with Godself and the world. God's ideal is that we live in this interconnected way, connected with the Creator and creation. This way of believing points us to the beauty always present alongside this world's ever-present struggles. If we can begin to see through an incarnational lens—seeing God in all things—it can help us cultivate awe.

———— *&* ————

Author Dacher Keltner studies awe. He sums up this feeling as our response to powerful things that are obscure, vast, and mysterious. We feel awe when we experience something beyond our typical frame of reference. Awe is not the same as joy. According to a *New York Times* article featuring Keltner and his research, "Our bodies respond differently when we are experiencing awe. . . . We make a different sound, show a different facial expression."[7] The vastness of the awe-filled experience makes us feel small and fills us with wonder.[8]

Feeling awe has numerous benefits for our minds and bodies, including calming inflammation, reducing pain perception, and calming down our brain's stress center.[9] Awe also stimulates the release of oxytocin, the "love" hormone that promotes bonding.[10]

Psychologically, awe helps calm the inner critical voices that tell us we're in some way not good enough. Awe quiets this negative self-talk by deactivating the part of our brain's cortex involved in how we perceive ourselves.[11]

Thankfully, awe is something we can develop and is not confined to nature. In his research, Dr. Keltner studied people's understanding of awe in twenty-six countries and found eight types of awe that are available to all of us. They include music, moral beauty (noticing kindness between people), birth and death, visual design, spirituality, and yes, nature. Awe also comes from what Keltner calls "collective effervescence." This feeling comes when we experience beautiful things in group settings when we are moving as one. We can feel this kind of awe at a sporting event or music concert, on a dance floor, in worship, in a choir, or during a group run.[12] I have experienced this kind of awe at one of my particular loves—musicals. I have known awe while sitting in a New York audience and in local theaters because God provides us all unique gifts and God delights in us when we experience one another's gifts together.

We feel awe when we are fully present in worldly beauty, and yet awe is otherworldly. Awe is here and it's transcendent.

I believe that is because God is here and transcendent. I believe experiencing awe is to experience the Divine. Awe helps us to connect to the God who is both universal & personal. When we recognize God in all things, experience how big this universe is, and realize how God still cares about us, we feel awestruck. When we live our life in such a way, when we practice noticing God in all things, it leaves us in awe.

As Richard Rohr puts it, *"God loves things by becoming them. God loves things by uniting with them, not by excluding them."*[13]

We can forget that the Bible is a relatively new creation. If we turn to Psalms of Orientation, how did these writers experience God? In religious settings, yes, and also in the clapping rivers, the singing mountains, and the handiwork of God's glorious skies. Then, God loved us so God became one of us.[14] He walked with us, healed us, suffered with us, grieved with us, rejoiced with us, and showed us the way to follow Him even when He left this earth.

Experiencing awe helps us become less self-preoccupied and instead shifts us into a more collective mindset, researchers have found. We engage with social groups more if we experience awe than if we lack awe in our lives.[15] Awe does not erase our problems, yet it can help lessen our stress by changing our brains and by holding our problems in light of our shared humanity. One of the ways we can practice gratitude in times of stress is to cultivate awe.

I believe awe is available to all of us. I believe awe is available to you—no matter where you live, no matter what you do—no matter what. When you believe God is in all things, you don't have to go very far to experience awe. Because God is in the theater, on the basketball court, in the notes of your favorite song playing on the radio, and in the paintings hanging in the Met and your town's local galleries. Can you begin to imagine it? God is with you now. God is in creation outside your window and God is in every person, including you. When you see God all around—when you can see God's expression of love in you and through you—you can experience awe. To experience awe is to feel both small & held. When you experience awe, you feel grateful to be here, grateful to have air in your lungs, grateful to be alive. You are alive. God is alive in you. God is alive in your neighbor across the street and in your child down the hallway. Awe may not be available to you every moment of the day, but it is waiting for you.

———— & ————

Andy and I had a choice. We could let the scenery of the bubbling geysers, peaking mountains, and wandering bison flow right past us. We could let our stress take over the day. Instead, we lived with it.

After exploring the Upper Geyser Basin, it was time to take our seats to watch Old Faithful erupt. Awe. I felt it. I looked around at the hundreds of tourists, mostly from different countries, and I felt awe in that too. We are all knowingly or unknowingly looking for what is both here and what is not. For what is known and what is unknown. We are all searching for something outside of ourselves, that thing that makes us feel how small we are and how big this universe is. We all want to experience the glory of this earth and what is not of this earth. We all want to get close to the mystery. And when we do, we stand and watch. Our eyes meet the flowing water. We get quiet. We gasp at the wonder of it all. We feel awed.

This mysterious God is faithful not by rescuing us from all our misfortunes. Instead, God's faithfulness is in the work that is all around us, below us, above us, and in us. This God sings to us by what we see aboveground and is also doing things we cannot see below. This God sets the forces in motion to heat the elements running below the surface. This God put systems in place so that the waters bubble and brew. This God may not come through on our set timetable, but sometimes delights us when those things we prayed for actually *do* happen right on time. One day, we may even look back and feel grateful for the times when things took a bit longer. Because we realize it was in those times of waiting that we became a bit more like the One who first breathed us into existence.

Andy and I had knots in our stomachs at different points in our day in Yellowstone & we were mesmerized by God's creation—an outpouring of Godself. As we drove from one point of beauty to another, we were reminded that life is complicated. Beauty is complicated. Some of the most beautiful moments in life—weddings, births, graduations—are not pure joy because there is an element of sadness in them. They hold beginnings & ache of endings; life will never quite be the same. Beauty is not the absence of the unsightly, but it's often the intertwining of harsh and soft, dull and bright, structured and unstructured components that awaken our hearts. It's the wildness of it all that makes us feel alive, that reminds us that this kind of beauty cannot be by chance. Instead, this beauty is a product of an artist who cannot be contained. Just as this artist created a masterpiece out of this mysterious blue and green jewel we call home, God makes a masterpiece out of our evolving lives.

——————— & ———————

When we arrived back home in Florida, the floor of my sticky kitchen did not feel as holy as the grounds of Wyoming. But I knew that it was. I told my child the truth—that this anxiety might be around for a while. That we would get them the professional help they needed. & I asked them to try to do one thing: to be present for the joy available every day. I asked them to try, even though the anxious thoughts may be flowing beneath the surface, to be fully present in the lighter parts of the school day that didn't have to do with work. To listen and allow themselves to laugh at the lunchroom jokes, to really play and even compete in the games at recess, to be awake to that more obvious kind of beauty. They told me they would try. Some days were harder than others. So too it goes for us. Some days we recognize God in our morning prayer times, and sometimes we struggle to connect. Sometimes, we see God in the flowing river near our home, and sometimes the sight connects to our brain but not to our heart. Sometimes we can pause in the middle of a difficult day and remember that all may not be right, but many things are. And sometimes heavy things are just heavy. So we keep trying.

When we make it a practice to notice God in creation, God in all people, God all around, we recognize the beauty still present in this world and in our own lives. This wild, vast, mysterious God does not make all things beautiful in an instant, but over time. God may not erase the unsightly but creates beauty in the middle of the heated conditions and our lives. We can breathe in (this stress is heavy) & breathe out (beauty is still here). Because Love is still here.

I do not need to go to the mountains to experience God. I will keep going when I can because it is an intentional way to experience awe. However, the real work is to cultivate awe right where I stand—on the shores of my sandy beach, in the backyard with my kids, in the bedroom of a struggling child—reminding them that yes, life is hard, & beauty is still here.

———— *&* ————

When it comes to our circumstances, on the surface, it may look like nothing is happening. That old geyser might look the same today as it did yesterday. But we know somehow, in ways we can't see, in ways we don't understand, God is at work below. We know the water is heating and rumbling and being set in motion to burst forth with life. Even if this particular stress is here to stay, so too is God.

You can move forward with the stress *&* you can take note of the way the sun still glistens off the oak leaves above. You can acknowledge the stress in your body *&* you can allow yourself to cheer on your favorite sports team. You can be honest about the mental toll *&* pause in a parking lot when a song comes on that seems to be playing just for you. You can live—knowing your problems are real, your stress is difficult to deal with, and God's goodness does not run out.

We may have been taught to believe that the way to experience God in the middle of our stress is to follow a set of rituals set out by religious authorities or influencers. If we just follow these steps, then we will be rescued. Then we will experience the presence of God here on earth. But the very nature of awe is that it comes by way of mystery. Because God is purposefully mysterious. So we take these tired feet, minds, and hearts to the ball field and the workplace, and on the way, we practice noticing. We notice how this stress is affecting our health. We notice how our jaws are having a hard time relaxing. We notice how our necks are stiff with worry. We ask for help. We take the help offered.

———— *&* ————

We notice how somehow God is meeting us too.

Dr. Keltner recommends cultivating awe by doing these things:

- Paying attention, avoiding distraction, and being present.
- Focusing on moral beauty between others. I would add participating in this beauty for yourself too!
- Choosing unfamiliar paths—like taking a different route to work, choosing a new restaurant, or taking a trip to somewhere new to you.[16]

I will add this: You can work on becoming a person who is easily delighted.

I remember eating Christmas dinner at Andy's parents' home in Georgia years ago. Being from Florida, I had never had a white Christmas. Georgia is not known for white Christmases either. But as we sat around the dinner table, fat, fluffy snowflakes poured from the sky. They all kind of made fun of me as I couldn't stop talking about it. I was utterly delighted.

I admit that I may be moody. I get stressed often & I have become a person who delights in things both big and small. I have become a person who walks my dog every day because it's good for her and good for me and because I love to feel the coastal breeze on my skin first thing in the morning. I have become a person who makes a habit of taking a big inhale and exhale as I drive over the causeways near our home, making sure my eyes catch the sunlight glittering off the river if only for a moment. I have become a person who may not experience awe every single day, but I do make a point to be delighted. Because that is a choice. Eventually, mysteriously, that delight becomes so all-encompassing, so powerful, so married with God and myself that it crosses over into awe.

This is possible for you too. You can see God all around. You can see God in a kind co-worker, in a child who still wants a bedtime story, and in the dancing stream you pass on the way to school drop-off. You can notice. And when you do, you will see how even here, even with the pressure building and building, beauty is still here. God is still in the business of surprising us with the depths to which love can go. God surprises us by bringing new life out of what seems dormant, out of those places that have looked and felt the same for so long. There God was; there God is. God, who is "over all and through all and in all,"[17] has been there all along. God is in all things. God so loved the world, He became a part of it. He died for it. He came back for it.

He is here now.

How delightful.

It's a mystery that we will never have all the answers to.

But we do our best to enter the mystery every day.

And when we do, we sometimes get the honor of standing in awe.

FURTHER READING

Psalm 8

❖ REFLECTION ❖

Write down two or three memories of experiencing awe. What were you doing? Who were you with? Consider ways you can cultivate awe in your daily life. Reflect on how this practice of really noticing God all around can help you pause and be grateful.

& GRATITUDE PRACTICE

What is stressing me now?

Where can I currently see beauty in my life?

What has been the greatest stress of my life?

Looking back, I can see goodness at work during that time in this way:

The hardest thing about stress for me is:

Stressful periods have taught me this about myself, this about God, this about life:

2

Longing & Grateful

LATE 2019
SAN ANTONIO, TEXAS

IT WAS SATURDAY—the most dreaded day of my week. It wasn't always that way, of course. Saturday is perhaps universally agreed upon to be the very best day of the week— sandwiched between the responsibilities of yesterday and the lack of responsibilities on Sunday. However, Saturdays in Texas became familiar, too familiar.

Our three years in Texas were spent in a Disordered period, yet we hit this spot of normalcy within it. We were in that space between Disorder and Reorder, which felt a lot like Order. We spent the latter part of our three-year Texas residency with threats to our children's health still present, but further away than they once were. We still had doctor appointments multiple times a month, sometimes even multiple times a week, but not every day.

Andy and I made a point to make Friday night a date night in. I had free respite care through the military, but if I wanted to be an author, I needed to use those hours to build a social media presence and write my book. So I did. This meant that instead of getting babysitters on Friday night, we had this routine: I scoured Pinterest for new recipes—something our three children under five would never eat. After the kids were fed their meal, Andy bathed them while I chopped, sautéed, and stirred. We kissed the kids goodnight and had dinner by candlelight at my grandmother's hand-me-down kitchen table. We reconnected, we laughed, we watched a show. The Friday nights looked similar to one another but there was always a bit of variety added in with a new recipe, a new show, a new topic to explore. We made it special. Friday nights were sacred.

But then Saturday rolled around and it was always the same. Saturday morning cartoons and sweet cuddles, yes. Then the YMCA where Andy would exercise, the kids went to onsite daycare, and I would pull up my laptop and write on a wobbly table next to burnt coffee, sweeteners, and powdered creamer.

We would sometimes splurge and pick up Chick-fil-A on our way home. We'd eat lunch, then put the youngest two down for a nap, while entertaining our oldest one. Then the boys would wake up, and all three would run out to jump in the outdoor bounce house my in-laws bought for them. Nearly all the pictures from this time have the backdrop of a bright yellow, green, and red playscape that entertained the kids and allowed us to keep our sanity.

There was nothing bad about Saturdays. It's just that we were not the adventurous parents who could handle trips to a café, a museum, or a theme park regularly. Our son with Down syndrome was a flight risk with serious impulse-control issues. Even if he had none of those issues, getting out and creating variety in the trenches of the toddler years is hard. Saturdays were not bad. Saturdays were a reprieve from the very early school days, therapy appointments, and doctor visits. Saturdays were quite adorable, with living-room dance parties and bike rides, & Saturdays were mundane. Life was better than it had been. We were not being squeezed by the unexpected as before. Instead, life was becoming the opposite of unexpected. It was predictable.

-------- *&* --------

When life hums along, when days become laced with sameness, it's a privilege. I don't say this to condemn my younger self. Those mundane days were full of goodness and oftentimes very long. When we get to a place where life doesn't have too many stressors (acknowledging here once more that there will always be a few), it is a gift. When we are privileged to live in Ordered times, we have more time to wonder, more space to dream, and we can begin to long. In Disordered times, we also long. We long for the pain to be relieved; we long for the grieving to end, for justice, for redemption. In Ordered times, we long for something different, or perhaps something more.

To long is to yearn for something outside of ourselves. To long is to be in want. During this transition from Disorder to Reorder, I longed for excitement to enter my life again. I longed for ease—like not having to be so hypervigilant about my boys' safety or having to block off an extra thirty minutes just to get into the car. I was in my thirties and I longed for a new career. I realized that going back to my former career as a television news reporter/anchor would not fit my life as a military spouse who moved frequently and as a mother of two medically complex children. I saw writer friends of mine online whose platforms exploded and who landed book deals—while my online spaces grew slowly and a book deal was a distant dream. I was grateful for my children's improving health, grateful that in these hard toddler years, I had a partner I adored. I was grateful & I was longing. Before writing this chapter, I asked my longtime pastor and mentor, Dan, What do people struggle with when life is relatively good? I was surprised by how quickly he answered me: temptation. We can be tempted by many things when life is good—including being tempted into thinking we are the sole reason our life is as good as it is. We can quickly become the kings and queens of our kingdoms. We also can be tempted by the superficial. We can be tempted to long for what our neighbor is wearing, or for a different car in the school drop-off line, or to escape to where our friends have traveled. We can be tempted into thinking that happiness, or more happiness, is just another purchase or milestone away. If only we can get there. Then we will catch up. Then we will surpass our neighbor's worthiness. Then we will be more. Our lives will be more.

———— *&* ————

"[It] is the worst thing that ever happened to me." That quote is not from someone who suffered the death of a loved one or who received a tough diagnosis, but they are the words of Billie Bob Harrell Jr.[1] Billie Bob won over $31 million by buying a winning lottery ticket in 1997. After spending, donating, and giving his money away, he was faced with bankruptcy and divorce. He took his own life almost two years after winning the jackpot.[2]

Most of us long for more money to buy things, to afford trips, and for our own financial security. Yet studies have shown that income affects human well-being but only up to a certain point. The positive benefits to our emotional well-being level off once earnings reach $75,000 annually. (This study was conducted in 2010, so roughly $110,000 in 2024.) Once we reach a certain salary threshold, we don't become less stressed or happier. Our well-being levels off.[3]

We humans have what psychologists call *impact bias,* which can show up as a tendency to overestimate how good (or bad) we will feel in the future and the effect current events will have on that. We have this in part because of *focalism,* the "tendency to place too much emphasis on a single factor" when making predictions or judgments.[4] When we think about a future event, we tend to forget the other factors in our lives that will simultaneously play out alongside this desired future event.[5]

In a famous study, psychologist Dan Gilbert and his team asked professors at the University of Texas how they thought they would feel if they earned tenure at their university using a seven-point happiness scale. The professors predicted they would feel a happiness level of six. In actuality, after the surveyed professors did earn tenure, they reported experiencing a happiness level of only five. Professors also predicted that if they did not receive tenure, they would feel a 3.4 on the happiness scale; in reality, the professors who did not earn tenure felt a whole point better when getting bad news, reporting a feeling a 4.7 on the happiness scale.[6] Also in the study, participants overestimated the duration of their reactions to the breakup of a romantic relationship, negative personality feedback, rejection from a prospective employer, and even an account of a child's death. Gilbert sums up the findings this way: "The good things won't be as good, the bad things won't be as bad as your mind leads you to believe."[7]

Psychologists call this phenomenon *hedonic adaptation*. We can't remain at a seven out of seven on the happiness scale because if we do, our emotional system isn't doing its job. Gilbert explains that we are meant to come back to baseline so that this system can guide us to the next good thing.[8]

We are built to long. But our longings are not meant to be satisfied in a way that prevents us from ever longing again. "Happily ever after" really is for fairytales. We can experience extreme levels of happiness after a longing is achieved, but we cannot stay there forever.

We are all longing to quell a grief over something we sometimes cannot even name. We may long to climb up the societal ladder with success and possessions. We may long to achieve the perfect physique because that is what we think will help us stand out. We may long to fill emotional emptiness by chasing one fun experience after another.

I wonder what it is that you long for right now. Are you longing to be promoted at work? Are you longing to fit in better—or perhaps to stand out more? Are you longing for better relationships, for more quality time with people you love? Do you long for more ease, or more possessions? I wonder if you are longing over a dream you can't shake— something that is trying to lead you home. No matter what it is you are longing for, you are not alone. We were made to long. Yet, this constant pull is calling us to dig deeper than what social media and self-help culture try to sell. If only we go to the right well to find it.

&

She lived many lives. Today was just another long day in one of her later years. It was hot, too hot. Sweat beaded on her upper lip as the sun scorched the place of her collective past, a place of her dreaded present. *She knew she would be alone. That's why she went at the height of the sun's unrelenting blaze. She could not bear the stares. She could not be reminded once more that she did not belong. Five times she was married. Five times she was left. She could not leave—didn't have the right. She was the one left out in the cold of the night—wondering what man would take her in next. She may have had the comfort once more of a roof over her head, but that did not protect her from the duties that called. She still would have to go back into the heat of the day, back to the well. She could not survive their stares, but she could not survive without the water's life-giving force. So she went once more.*

This time, she wasn't alone. A man was there. A Jewish man. Such men had called her unworthy her whole life. But not this man. Instead, He asked her for a drink. She was confused. Why was He even speaking to her? She was used to stares, but she was not used to being seen.

He went on to tell her that this water, the water she was drawing, would never quench her thirst. Not fully. Only He had water that would make it so she would never thirst again. Only He could offer the kind of water that would well up and create a spring. Only He could satisfy her longings. With Him, she would never be rejected, kicked out, on the outside looking in. With Him, she would have a home. With Him, she would be fed. With Him, no matter what the world told her, she would have His truth living inside her—she was worthy after all. She was worthy because she was His.[9]

There's an encounter Jesus has in the Bible commonly referred to as "The Woman at the Well." Maybe you were taught the woman at the well was an adulteress or even a prostitute due to her marriage history. (Or possibly the church created this narrative to discredit a woman as being the first citywide evangelist.)[10] We don't know this woman's whole story. But we do know she lived in a patriarchal society—one in which she was considered her husband's property. We know she did not have the right to divorce her husbands.[11] Ultimately, we know that in one way or another, she suffered. We know that later in her encounter with Jesus, she asked about worship. We know she was thirsty to survive, yes, and thirsty for God—a God to whom the gatekeepers had told her she did not have access. Nevertheless, a God she did not stop searching for.

This woman was marginalized by the larger society; men rarely spoke to women in public, and this woman was an outcast because she was a Samaritan. Jews did not like Samaritans because they were an ethnic group descended from intermarriages between Jews and Assyrians, which went against Jewish law. She was also perhaps even outcast by her husbands and her own people. It was this woman with whom Jesus decided to have the longest theological conversation recorded in the Bible.[12] It was this woman to whom He revealed His true identity for the first time.

Whereas most Jews would take the long way around Samaria when traveling, Jesus went right through it. He had to, according to John 4:4. Just a chapter earlier, we learn that God so loved the world[13]—and we learn why Jesus came. Here we see that He came for the oppressed Samaritan woman. He came for us all. Jesus revealed to her who she was and in doing so revealed who we are too: We are people who experience heartache and pain, who know this world cannot be all there is; we are people who long for something different. Jesus revealed her identity to reveal His own. He is the only One who can fulfill the longings of our hearts—both the ones we can name and the ones we don't have language for. He was the One they were waiting for. He was the One who came not to condemn the world, but to save it.[14]

The woman couldn't contain herself. He knew her. He knew them all. She had to go tell everyone she knew. The wait was over. Jesus turned this woman who intimately knew pain into the first evangelist. This was her redemption. This is our redemption too. She spread the word of Jesus' identity. In doing so, she drank from the well of living water. In our doing so, God teaches us how to fulfill that emptiness we feel that has us wanting more. It's never found in a thing. Our deepest longings can only be satisfied by the One who breaks through barriers to find us, who loves us just as we are, and who calls us into good purposes.

I do not think we will ever feel fully satisfied here on earth. God designed us in such a way that we are meant to long and keep longing. What a relief. The act of longing is not an act of ingratitude. We are meant to dip down into this spring that lives inside of us, drink, and then keep walking in the ways He walked. We walk in the ways that do not avoid hard things but go right through them. We walk in the way of seeking out the forgotten. We find the lives we long for when we walk in the ways of love.

&

We were built to long, but how do we deal with modern longings following the ancient ways of Jesus? How can we long while being grateful for all we have, being grateful for all of God's goodness that is present both inside and outside our circumstances? I don't have an action plan. I don't know what Jesus would think about our longing to move to a different house to get our kids into a better school district; I don't know what He would think about our deep desire to make a big career move. I don't know. I believe the best we can do is to run our longings through a Jesus-filled strainer and see what gets stuck and what comes out the other side. Are our longings fueled by love?

Can we get there by walking in the ways of mercy instead of dominance? Are our intentions pure of heart or influenced by consumerism? Will our longings help us live into the fullest version of ourselves—the version God conceived long ago? Because if so, they matter. Because we matter. Our transformation matters. Once we know we want to continue on this path of going after this longing, we can practice two seemingly conflicting habits: prospection and gratitude.

Prospection is our ability to imagine the future, or more precisely, our ability to simulate multiple futures. Thinking about the future can trigger anxiety, and positive thinking about the future can actually backfire.[15] However, there is growing evidence that thinking about the future can help make our lives more meaningful and help us accomplish our goals—if we do it well.[16] So how do we use prospection over our good longings for our benefit? Mental contrasting.

A study conducted by New York University asked students to mentally contrast their fantasies about benefitting from their study program while also considering aspects of the program that could impede their progress. What researchers found was that positive expectations of the future only worked in the students who were assigned to compare their present situation with their future desires.[17] Results from a later study found that mental contrasting was key in achieving goals because it gives us the energy to break through the inevitable barriers we will have to face.[18]

We cannot forget that life will play out alongside reaching that goal. We must not go after our big longings for the big moment because that big moment will never be as grand as we have built it up to be in our minds—not even winning the lottery. The big moment will come, and there will still be school pickups and grocery runs right alongside that long-awaited event. This part, right here, the part where we work as we long is a hard & good part of the process. We can look to the future with hope—knowing we have a God who has already gone before us & we must look at the lives we have right now with the God who is with us in the waiting. We must not skip over the goodness of God, the goodness of our lives here and now.

You can long for and work toward a career change & find something to be grateful for at your current place of work.

You can long for excitement in your life & keep your eyes open to precious moments within the mundane.

You can long to make a difference in a big way & you can look for ways to make a difference in your day-to-day with small acts of kindness.

Looking back, I can see some of my longings were very good. I was trying to live into the fullness of myself. I could envision a future of how I was supposed to bring a bit of healing into the world in the way God designed me. I knew getting there would not be easy. At times, I was impatient. At times, it was heartbreaking. At times, I failed. Yet, by taking steps and by not letting go of the vision I believe I co-created with God—and ultimately by Grace—that big longing to write books finally came to fruition.

However, there were other longings I could have handled better. I wish I had known a phrase I learned just before my first book was published, a phrase that has since helped me practice real gratitude because it helps me to be honest about my longings and reminds me that there is beauty in this phase I am in. The phrase is this: It's not my turn.[19]

I wish I had known this phrase in the latter part of those Texas years when I was typing away at the YMCA by the burnt coffee and later going home and changing diapers and cutting grapes into two.

Back when I wanted life to be a bit more exciting again—it wasn't my turn.

It was not my turn to sit by the pool.
It was not my turn for nights out on the town.
It was not my turn to take that risk.
It was not my turn to volunteer.
It was not my turn to travel.

This phrase has served me well. Knowing it's not my turn helps me to take a deep breath and focus on where my life is right now. To look at the hard & the good with clear eyes. To know where I hope to go and know all I have right here, right now.

It was my turn to go through a huge mental and spiritual growth period.
It was my turn to use the quietness of those years to dive deeper into study.
It was my turn to deepen my marriage.
It was my turn to cherish baby cuddles.
It was my turn to do the slow and steady work of making my dream come true—and the slowness and steadiness of it did make the achievement sweeter once it finally happened.

It is not our turn for everything. It never is. It is our turn for some things.

Even if it is not your turn to go after or experience the deep longing you have inside of you, that doesn't mean your turn won't come. You should know, if your longings are fulfilled, that satisfaction, that happiness, is not a place you can camp out on forever. You aren't designed that way; none of us is.

We visit the mountaintops, and when we do, we point our face toward the sun. We say thank you, knowing we did not get there on our own. Eventually, the sun will have to set. When it does, we go back to the spring again.

We drink from the living water, knowing that it will sustain us in the lives we have right now.

&

We drink from this water, knowing it will fuel us for the lives we do not have yet.

We keep coming back, back to the spring, back to the water that flows and flows right alongside us with the lives we have and the lives we will one day live.

We drink, knowing this water will not grant us our every desire.

We drink, knowing this water is the only thing that can fulfill us the best way possible this side of heaven.

We drink and say, "Thank you for sustaining me here. Thank you for guiding me toward my fullest self." We drink knowing we will always want more.

Further Reading

Psalm 33

❖ Reflection ❖

Write out your current longings. Try to filter them through a Jesus-filled strainer. Are there things that bring you closer to His ways of love and mercy? If so, write a second list of those longings, only. Mentally contrast where you want to be versus where you are now so you can begin to create a roadmap.

& GRATITUDE PRACTICE

I am longing for the day when:

I am grateful for this that I am learning in the waiting:

It's not my turn for:

I am grateful it is my turn for:

I am sad this past longing never came to fruition:

I am grateful for this I received instead:

3

Busy & Grateful

FOR A TIME, I wore it as a badge. Back in the 2010s it was common to list out all you did in a day or had to do and post it to social media. Some of us liked to show our little corners of the world just how *busy* we were. How very Western of us. Back then, my busyness was filled with TV interviews and calling sources to find the next big scoop. It was filled with weird hours and squeezing in dinner with Andy between newscasts. It was working Thanksgiving or Christmas—or sometimes both. But I was seen. I was putting in the time required to get to the top. In a society that wants us to do, do, do, in order to earn, earn, earn, so that we can buy, buy, buy, so we can be at the top of the ladder of success, busy can quickly become a way of life.

Today, my busyness is not what it was pre-kids nor what it was when my life was in Disorder. My busyness is still nothing to put in a social media post. It is not unique; it's just the makings of a life. My busyness might look a lot like yours: It's working two part-time jobs, going to work events with my husband, transporting kids to their mountain of activities, and it's trying to have meaningful conversations with them in the meantime. It's making dinner, cleaning up dinner, and trying not to collapse at the end of the day. It is the life I have mostly chosen. It's a life that I love & it's a life that is so very tiring.

It's not just me, or you, or the season of life we are in. About a quarter of the patients in my husband's orthodontic practice are adults, and although only a small percentage are retirees, he commonly hears the same thing from his older patients. They tell him they are busier in retirement than they were when they were working! No matter where we are in life, no matter how our days are filled, life can get busy.

In a study published in *Psychological Science* in 2010, researchers found that people who keep busy are more likely to remain happy than those who become idle.[1] In this study, researchers asked college students to take surveys about their schools. After completing the first survey, students could either drop it off outside the room they were in, then wait until the next survey was administered, or keep busy by dropping off the survey at a location that was about fifteen minutes away. The students who kept busy by dropping off the survey at the further location reported being happier than the students who did not. Researchers did a variation of this study in which students did not have a choice, but were assigned to drop off their surveys outside the room or at a location fifteen minutes away. Again, the students who had to go farther to drop off the survey reported being happier than those who sat idly.

Busyness makes us feel good & busyness can make us sick. Busyness is a sign of what neuroscientists call "cognitive over-load," a state that impairs our ability to learn, create, and control our emotions.[2] In 2018, Pew Research conducted a study on busyness and found that 74 percent of parents who had kids under the age of eighteen felt that at least sometimes, they were too busy to enjoy life.[3] Busyness can lead to stress, which we have already discussed can lead to mental and physical issues.

What do we do with a life that is so very busy?

What do we do with a life that is busy with things of our choosing and busy with things that are not?

How do we live the full life God wants us to live without getting overstuffed?

And what do we do when we are overstuffed?

How do we practice gratitude, an act that requires us to take notice, when our lives are so full?

In this chapter we will go over three ways to keep our busyness in check: delegation, empowered nos, and rest. In this way, we can better manage our busyness so we can live our full lives while also living with gratitude.

————— *&* —————

When the unexpected happened for the third time in three years with my youngest son's diagnosis I will tell you about later, I was busy with things not of my choosing. I was busy with the forty-five-minute commute to the hospital across town multiple times a month. I was busy with therapy appointments for both of my boys, with trying to teach our oldest to read. I was busy with trying to cook dinner during the witching hour and a husband in residency. I was busy in ways no one would notice. My busyness was largely a means to survive.

Yet, I was also busy by my yeses. I was not quite the stay-at-home-mom type, but that was the life that made the most sense for our family at the time due to all the boys' appointments and care. So I filled up my free time with work. I said yes to a board position for a nonprofit and to a freelance public relations gig. I said yes to putting all my extra hours into building online spaces but without a clear direction of why I was investing my time there. My busyness was a means to survive, yes. It was also a means for my fulfillment because I was drowning in responsibilities that come with being a parent of children with medical complexities. I needed something of my own. I would leave for an appointment, return home, and instead of taking a breath while the boys were napping, I was grinding. I would pull up my laptop and squeeze in an hour or two of work during nap time. When the boys awoke, I would squeeze more productivity in on my phone. "Me time" was work time. I didn't realize that all of my yeses meant I was saying no to much. I was saying no to rest, I was saying no to being present with my kids when we finally had downtime in the day, I was saying no to being quiet enough to discern where my heart was leading me.

Saying yes can lead to new opportunities, to self-discovery; and it can lead us to possibilities we never thought possible. However, if we say yes too often, we can believe the false narrative that it is all up to us. We can believe the PTA simply won't run unless we say yes to taking on that officer role the president asked us to. We can believe that if we don't say yes to working during our family time, the project won't get done the correct way. We can believe that we alone are responsible for everything and everyone we come in contact with. Our identity can quickly become attached to our output.

Yes is powerful; yes can help us live more bravely and even more tenderly. Our Creator desires for us to live a full life, and full life requires us to say yes. & we must recognize this truth: Any time we say yes to something, it means we are saying no to something else. We must be careful with our yeses & we must get comfortable with saying no. We must get comfortable with delegating.

Delegation

There is a story in Exodus 18 in which Moses, the leader of the Israelite nation, is confronted by his father-in-law, Jethro. From morning until evening, Moses worked in his role of judge among his people. Jethro noticed how busy Moses was. He asked him, "Why do you alone sit as judge while all these people stand around you from morning until evening?"[4] Moses told him it was because the people depended on him to seek God's will, explaining that whenever the people had a dispute, he decided between the parties in accordance with God's decrees.

Jethro was frank, "What you are doing is not good. You and these people who come to you will only wear yourselves out. The work is too heavy for you; you cannot handle it alone."[5]

What Moses was doing was not good. It wasn't good for him. It wasn't good for the people who had to wait for his guidance. We are meant to carry much, and we are meant to help carry the burdens of others, but we cannot carry everything.[6] The weight is simply too heavy. We suffer when we get too busy, and the people who depend on us suffer too.

Jethro went on to tell Moses that he needed to delegate. He needed to appoint people to share the load. He was not the only capable person among his people. It can be tempting to think we are though, can't it?

It can also be tempting to think only we know how to handle our children's needs, only we can manage our family's schedule, and only we can get the job done right. When we believe it is all up to us, we can get so very busy. When we do this, we hurt ourselves. When we do this, we hurt those who love us. And we hurt others who are missing out on the opportunity to play a part. We deny others room for growth, we deny others purpose, and we deny them that good kind of busyness.

Moses listened to Jethro's advice and delegated. He set up a panel of judges to carry the load. He laid the foundation for the judicial system that Israel would thrive under for years. Moses' life improved, and the lives of his people improved when he shared his burden and asked others to carry it with him. He might never have gotten there without an outsider looking in. He would not have gotten there without saying no to some of his busyness so he could eventually say yes to the full life God wanted for him.

Although I was busy in Texas with things not of my choosing, I was also busy with too many things that were by choice. I had little direction because my identity was being reformed. My life was being reformed. I didn't know where I was heading, so I started saying yes to every opportunity that came my way, whether I wanted it or not. I needed a Jethro. Thankfully, I found one.

&

Empowered Yeses and Nos

During our time in Texas, we hosted a bi-monthly Bible study at our house. Each study member was in a similar phase of life. We all had very young children, and we were all busy. We rotated who brought the main course and who brought a side, dessert, or paper goods. We broke bread together alongside our gaggle of children. Then we watched a video study for a half hour and had a discussion afterward, all while a babysitter watched our wild brood upstairs or outside.

We eventually landed on a very old sermon series by Andy Stanley about discerning the will of God. I'm talking *cheesy skits before the preacher preached* old. So we obviously fast-forwarded through those to the meat of the message. The fourth week of the series was my Jethro moment.

Stanley said, "The clearer the vision, the fewer the options, the easier the decision."[7] He used the picture atop a puzzle box to describe how we need to have a vision for our lives and use that vision to guide our decisions.

I realized something: I had no vision for my life. I had checked off the major boxes. I had received an education, worked in my dream field; I got married and had kids. But now what? Without direction, I started saying yes to every request and every opportunity that came my way. For a time, those yeses helped me discover more about myself and more about what I wanted out of life in the aftermath of the un-expected. However, it was time to create a vision for my life. It was time to create a new vision for our family, to get clear on our values. It was time to focus on one professional endeavor and start marking some boundaries. It was time to start saying no.

Vanessa Patrick, author of *The Power of Saying No*, coined the term *the empowered no*. An empowered no stems from our identity and gives voice to our "values, priorities, prefer-ences, and beliefs."[8] Thankfully, I was starting to get know my new self—the self who emerged from the shedding and the rebirth that takes place after life as you know it ends, and then begins. Thankfully, I knew myself well enough to start living out of empowered nos and empowered yeses. I think you know yourself well enough to do so as well. You don't have to wait to have it all figured out to create and live out of a vision. You just need to know who you are and have an idea of who you would like to become.

I was still busy. But I became busy with things that fit into my vision and let go of the things that did not. That vision included my marriage being at the top of my priority list, a home where our kids felt close to us and each other, a career as an author and speaker, one where we would continue to fight for an inclusive world for our son with a disability and one where the love of God would hopefully shape all our nos and all our yeses. I let go of a nonprofit board position. I quit my freelance PR job. I started saying no to volunteer requests that I had previously said yes to. & I continued to say yes to investing in my studies and writing daily, yes to family dinners (nearly) every night, and yes to advocacy courses so we could be the best advocates for our son with a disability.

There is a line from the Old Testament book of Nehemiah that hangs on my wall. Nehemiah left his prestigious position as a cupbearer for the Persian King Artaxerxes to lead a group of Jews back to Jerusalem to rebuild the city walls. In doing so, Nehemiah led a physical revival to the city and also a spiritual one.[9] In chapter 6, Nehemiah's enemies try to convince him to come down from building the wall to have a meeting. Nehemiah sent messengers with this reply, "I am doing a great work and I cannot come down."[10] When I look at these words, I am reminded that I am to keep building and living out of the vision I believe I have co-created with God and my family. To do so, I can only carry the pieces that are meant for my life. It is a great work, and I can only keep doing this great work if I avoid picking up pieces that are not mine to carry.

Now that I find myself in an Ordered period, I know it is time to redraw the vision again. It is time to get clear about what we want for our family life as our children are getting older, to get clear about what we want out of life now that the big goals have been met. It's time to look at where God has planted us, to evaluate the gifts we have been given and how we are supposed to use them. It's time to think about what God's highest desire is for us both inside and outside the walls of our home. It is time to recommit to seeking the life God wants for all of us—one marked by love.

We should never be so busy that we miss the goodness of God right where we stand. It's not that we won't be busy. It's that we should never get so busy that we stop noticing. When we live out of our vision, when we delegate, when we are careful with our yeses and our nos, we can be busy & awake to beauty.

We can take our kids to the ball fields and notice how their giggles are contagious as a smile spreads across our face. We can build that project at work and feel grateful that this effort is adding up to something meaningful. We can drive to an appointment with our partner and feel the warmth of their hand atop our own and whisper a simple prayer of thanks.

As we draw up this vision alongside our Creator, our partners, and our families, let us remember to have empowered yeses and empowered nos. If we find ourselves in that 74 percent of parents who are too busy to enjoy life, it's time to start mapping out what we want that picture atop the puzzle box of our lives for the next five to ten years to look like. Let's have honest conversations with our partners and support systems about what is working and what is not. Let's take care of our share, delegate where we can, and let go of what is not meant for us. Let's remember that when we say yes to too many things, we might be saying no to the things that matter most.

If the requests we receive to volunteer or work late or the pressure we feel to enroll our kids in one more activity or have our houses look Instagram-worthy at all times do not fit our values, priorities, beliefs, and that vision we have done our best to co-create with God, then let the words of Nehemiah ring in our ears: We are doing a great work and cannot come down.

> We cannot come down for things we feel pressured to do but that do not fit into our vision.
>
> We cannot come down for every volunteer opportunity.
>
> We cannot come down for work when it is time to be with our families.
>
> We cannot come down for unreasonable expectations of others.
>
> We cannot come down for unreasonable expectations we put on ourselves.
>
> We cannot come down for a life that is not intended for us to live.

Because when we do, we miss out on the life that makes us fully alive.

———— *&* ————

Rest

Jesus's life was one filled with inconvenient yeses. In the previous chapter, we explored His encounter with the woman at the well. We learn just how tired Jesus was before having that barrier-breaking conversation: He was so tired that he sat wearily by the well in the heat of the midday sun.[11] Once, after preaching all day, He went away with His disciples by boat to rest and eat, only to be greeted by a different crowd. Instead of recharging, He told this crowd the good news too.[12]

Jesus's life was marked by inconvenient yeses & Jesus often said no to get to those good yeses. Jesus often said no to what others expected of Him to fulfill the vision God had for His life and ministry. Jesus was busy & Jesus made it a habit to rest and to tap into God's love.

In the book of Mark, before Jesus preaches, serves, and heals, He goes to the wilderness to prepare for His ministry. Jesus started from a place of solitude, fasting, and prayer. Jesus made taking time to rest a habit, often to the confusion or even disappointment of His followers. In Mark 1:35–38, we read that Jesus woke up very early and went off alone to pray. His disciples didn't know where He was. They set out to look for Him and once they found Jesus, they exclaimed, "Everyone is looking for you!" Jesus responded by telling them His plans: that they were going to preach to the nearby villages. However, in order to start this next leg of His mission, He had to spend time alone with God.

Luke chapter 4 records Jesus healing Simon Peter's mother-in-law and then many more in Capernaum. Afterward, He went out to a solitary place again. The people went out looking for Jesus and found Him. They tried to convince Him to stay. But He told them, "I must proclaim the good news of the kingdom of God to the other towns also, because that is why I was sent."[13] Then He kept on preaching throughout Judea, but not before He rested. Luke 5:16 says Jesus often went to lonely places to pray. Not sometimes, not only when something pressing came up, but often. Resting with God was necessary for Jesus to do the work God was asking Him to do. Making a habit to retreat before we do the work we are called to do is necessary for us too.

Jesus's ministry was marked by yes, & to fulfill His mission of preaching and embodying the good news He often said no to the expectations of others. To say yes to His mission, Jesus needed to pray to the One who would fuel and sustain Him. Jesus never lost sight of His vision & He knew that to accomplish God's will for His life He had to rest. He had to intentionally make spending time alone with God a habit so He could live the life He was called to.

Jesus's busy life teaches us this: Resting in the love of God is necessary for us to carry out the lives we are called to live. Rest sustains us in our busyness. Rest is required for keeping our eyes open to the beauty within the busyness. Resting in our Creator requires our intention & adding it to our routine.

What does it take to add something new into our lives regularly? Research shows that around half of our daily actions are driven by repetition.[14] According to the *British Journal of General Practice*, habits are "actions that are triggered automatically in response to contextual cues that have been associated with their performance."[15] An example is how, when we get in a car, we automatically put on our seatbelt without much thought as to how or why we are doing it. Our brains like habits because they're efficient. Habits allow us to free up our brains for other tasks.

Unlike habits, routines are uncomfortable and require much effort. Nir Eyal, author of *Indistractible: How to Control Your Attention and Choose Your Life*, says many of us fail at establishing new habits because we try to skip the routine phase.[16] We have to do something routinely (which requires much thought and planning) for it to become a habit (which is our brain's automated response.)

Adding something to our already busy lives might seem contradictory, but Jesus' life shows us that adding rest to our lives is essential to live out the full lives God desires for us.

There is no one-size-fits-all for rest or prayer. Maybe waking up before the kids do to get thirty minutes of solitude will work for you. Maybe it's adding thirty seconds of prayer before every meal. Maybe it's praying a Psalm or liturgy before you fall asleep.

I can tell you that my prayer life has ebbed and flowed over the years.

At times, it feels life-giving & at times, God feels distant.

At times, prayer feels natural & at times, it feels forced.

At times, I feel God's presence through my prayer & at times, I have to hope I will feel God's presence tomorrow.

Sometimes, prayer leaves me with more questions than answers.

Sometimes, I think it's supposed to be that way.

What I have noticed about prayer is that when I am consistent, the prayer goes on. It's not just sitting on my couch in the early hours of the morning before my kids awake. It's a constant conversation throughout the day.

When I remember that God is with me at every turn of my busy day, I am much more likely to see God in all things. I am much more likely to see beauty in the busyness. I am much more likely to be honest about my stresses & I am much more likely to say thank you for things both big and small.

&

What do we do when we have already done all of these things? What if we have delegated, have already mapped out our vision, and have filtered our nos and our yeses through it? What if we already routinely pray and we are still so spent?

What do we do when we have done all we can to edit out what is unnecessary and are still overwhelmed by the necessary?

I think we rest in the humanness of Jesus. We not only recognize His divinity, but we also get up close to His humanity. We imagine walking the dusty roads He traveled for miles and miles; we imagine Him sitting against that well—spent. And we go back to the boat where He tried to get away and grieve the death of His cousin, only to be met with more people who needed Him.

> Jesus's life was busy & it was full of purpose.
> Jesus's life was busy & it was full of love.
> Jesus's life was busy & God was never far.
> Jesus's life was busy & He never stopped thanking
> God—for God's great work and before accomplishing
> great works through God.[17]

So too it can be with us.

Sometimes, in our busyness, we forget that we are living the life we hoped for. When the kids' schedules get too full, when I have to drop work because someone has a tummy ache, when the laundry pile gets too high, when the cooking every night frays my nerves, sometimes I forget. I can forget that I'm living the life I hoped for.

Because I hoped to have a minivan full of kids to transport to activities.

I hoped to have flexible work that I enjoy.

Although the laundry and cooking every day can get old, I wanted to have a house full of people to love and take care of.

& I do.

& this life is sometimes harder than I imagined it would be.

& it is also so very lovely.

What if we remember that the full schedules, laundry loads, dinner plates, and overall busyness are reminders—that this is in many ways the life we once hoped for?

& when our busyness is too much, may we be honest with the God who knows busy.

We pray to the God who sweat and wept and lived out many inconvenient yeses.

We thank Him for intimately knowing our tiredness & ask for rest.

& we ask Him to help us to keep going and to keep going well.

We pray we live into the vision God has for our lives.

We take steps to make sure our busyness reflects the life we want, not the life others expect us to live.

We ask for wisdom to recognize when busyness is the product of living into good purposes, for which we truly can be grateful, & when it has become a badge for others to admire.

May we know when we need to carry a heavier load & when it is time to ask someone to help shoulder it.

May we do & may we simply be.

May our yeses be plentiful & may we say no often with grace. Once we have done the sifting, may we remember this from our Teacher: A busy life can be hard & it can be good.

FURTHER READING

Psalm 131

❖ REFLECTION ❖

What is your five- to ten-year vision? How might filtering
your commitments through this vision help you to be busy
with worthy things and less busy with unworthy things?

& GRATITUDE PRACTICE

I am busy with these things I wish I could change:

I am grateful I can make a difference in this way:

This life I hoped for is harder than I thought it would be in this way:

This life I hoped for is beautiful in these ways I didn't expect:

I am tired from my busyness in this way:

I am thankful for the fullness in my life in this way:

4

Scared & Grateful

A LIFELONG FRIEND of mine and I had lived out one
unexpected circumstance after another almost in tandem.
It started with her—discovering an affair, and then divorce.
Then it was my turn—an unwanted move and an unexpected diagnosis. Then back to her—unexpected diagnosis
and grueling treatments. Then back to me—miscarriage and
another unexpected diagnosis. Then back to her—infertility.
For years, she and I walked along the shoreline, only to be
hit by a giant wave that pulled us out to the turbulent sea.
We would make our way back to the sand, back to something
resembling solid ground, only to be swept away once more.

Now she stood in my half-renovated kitchen, remarried
and mom to a sweet toddler. I giggled as she fed her child

guacamole by the spoonful. She laughed too. We made our way out of the ocean and up to the dunes. One of the ways dunes form is when the wind blows sand into a sheltered area behind an obstacle. Dunes are necessary to protect the coastline from erosion. For my friend, her husband's cancer was gone and her long-awaited child had been born. For me, after years of the unexpected, we landed back home in Florida. And yet, as a native Floridian, I know—dunes are always changing because of shifting sands.

She stood across from me as the smell of carne asada lingered. Dinner had been cleaned up (except for the guacamole!), dessert had been savored, and coffee had been sipped. Yet we lingered, like old friends do. We are bonded by lives that have been marked by the 10 percent. When doctors told us they were 90 percent sure the spot on the screen was benign or that surgery wouldn't be necessary, our lives fell into that dreaded less-likely space. My friend and I were connected by our parents taking us to the same preschool. We were connected by parents who cared enough about us to help us build a relationship. We are further connected by lives marked by the unexpected.

When you are connected by deep roots that intertwine, surface conversations can't last too long. She admitted to me that life was steady, life was good—life was even great now. Yet, it was hard to live into that good reality at times. It was hard to trust it. It was hard to live in the safety the dune provided, knowing shifting sands could change the landscape. It still felt as if another wave could come up higher than predicted, higher than it's supposed to; it still felt like she could be swept out to sea once more.

I paused, then nodded, and said, "Me too."

We admitted that when the slightest glimpse of the worst-case scenario appeared, we started to prepare. We would start building a fortress around us, forgetting that our circumstances are like the shifting sands. The winds come and change the scenery, sometimes with warning and sometimes out of the clear blue sky. I wrote in my first book that there is no way to prepare for what is unexpected and permanent. It's true. The unexpected will always shock you and pull you under and out. I knew that. Yet, her truth was at times my own. It's hard not to prepare for the worst even when you know from experience that nothing can protect your heart from the unexpected.

We once had the privilege of not knowing how fragile this life is. That privilege has been revoked. We know now. We know the truth: Life is so beautiful & life can be so scary.

------- *&* -------

Catastrophizing is a cognitive distortion displayed "when a person fixates on the worst possible outcome and treats it as likely, even when it is not."[1] Scientists have found it is most common for young adults between the ages of eighteen and thirty-five for two reasons. The first is because this is when our lives are the most uncertain. It's when many of us are picking schools, career paths, getting married, and buying homes for the first time.[2] The second is because our prefrontal cortex, the part of our brain that solves problems, is still developing in our twenties.[3] Multiple studies have also found that catastrophizing is also more common in people who have experienced traumatic or unsettling events in their lives. Experiencing something that once threatened us can lead us to believe something else threatening may happen in the future.[4]

Whether we have been through these Disordered scenarios that drag us out to sea, that in some way leave us fighting or feeling helpless, we all have what psychologists call *negativity bias.*

Negativity bias is our tendency to catalog and dwell on our negative experiences more than positive ones. It's why we remember the bite of negative feedback more intensely than we do the joy of positive feedback. I have a feeling it's why, when I entered the online writing world, other writers would tell me to never read the comments! Although the positive comments outnumber the negative ones, positive feedback sounds like a simple, pleasant, unmemorable melody. The negative comments are more like a blaring alarm. Even when you've punched in the code to turn it off, it still can randomly go off without warning. It's why we can enjoy a day full of good things, but one person with their words or actions toward us can have us categorizing the day as a bad one.

People tend to

- Remember traumatic experiences more than good ones.
- Think about negative things more than positive things.
- Make decisions based on negative data more than on positive information.[5]

Studies have even shown that "negative news is more likely to be perceived as truthful," perhaps because negativity takes up more of our attention, leading us to believe negative information is more valid.[6]

Negativity bias likely comes from our earliest ancestors, who had to pay attention to environmental threats to keep living.[7] Those who were more vigilant about possible danger had a higher chance of survival. This tendency also meant they were more likely to pass down the genes that made them more attentive to danger. Our brains focus on the negative to protect us.[8] But what do we do when we are not in immediate danger? What do we do with a God who tells us not to worry about tomorrow?[9] How can we live boldly when we have an instinct that urges us to play it safe? How do we embrace the fullness of our reality in an Ordered period while dealing with our thoughts that tell us, *Hold on, don't go too far, don't give too much?* How can we live knowing the truth that not one of us gets out of this life alive? How do we live scared & move forward anyway—and move forward well? How do we recognize beauty and goodness while knowing that suffering is part of the human condition and that if it hasn't come for us already, one day it will?

—————— *&* ——————

All major ancient civilizations developed tunneling methods. It is even probable that prehistoric people built tunnels to increase their living spaces.[10] The first excavated tunnel dates to 2200 BC Babylonia. There, historians uncovered a brick-lined pedestrian passage three thousand feet long under the Euphrates River that connected the royal palace with the temple.[11] Tunnels connect. Tunnels cut through the obstacles to help us arrive at our destination.

Tunnels have helped people progress, allowing us to travel and transport more efficiently. However, if we are not careful, we can remain stuck in tunneling. Tunnels connect, yes. But tunnels also take us below and block out the light above, giving us tunnel vision. Mind tunnels can make us hyperfocused on arriving because when we live scared, we can get addicted to destinations. So once we arrive, we can forget to enjoy the view. We're already scanning the environment, looking for new ways for things to go wrong, new ways to tunnel, instead of rising to the surface to enjoy the light—to enjoy just how far we have come. Instead, we create new tunnels there, moving on to the next thing.

A scarcity mindset is when our thoughts about not having enough affect how we move in the world. A scarcity mindset can occur in people who lack resources (finances, essentials, time) and in those who believe they lack resources.[12] This chapter is not aimed at those who have little, but at those of us who have much but have a hard time believing that we do. This chapter is also aimed at people like my friend and me, who have a hard time believing the good things won't be taken away from us.

Dr. Tabitha Kirkland, a psychologist and a professor at the University of Washington, says both "real and perceived scarcity can increase jealousy, stress and competition."[13] A scarcity mindset can captivate our minds so we can't think of other things. This mentality leads us to change our behaviors to short-term coping mechanisms, even when these behaviors can worsen our long-term outcomes.[14] Fixating on the things we believe we don't have enough of, or dwelling on the fear that the good things can disappear at a moment's notice, prevents us from being able to solve problems, retain information, control our impulses, or just be present.[15]

A scarcity mindset has us dipping below the surface, anxiously trying to arrive at the destination of more—more pleasure, more wealth, more power—often in the name of security. Scarcity mindset can have us living as if we don't have enough, believing we are not enough, believing it is only up to us to secure our future. When we live our lives with a scarcity mindset, we can get so hyper-focused on arriving that we forget to live. If we are not careful, we end up spending our lives in tunnels of our own making.

When we live with a scarcity mentality, the walls close in around us and we can't see the beauty that's present because we are narrowly focused on one thing. We might arrive at our desired destination but never believe it because we can't see our own feet in the dark. So, we go back to the tunnel and keep digging our way forward to the next destination, because then, only then, will we be safe. Only then will it be enough.

------ & ------

It was a good year, a good harvest. The land birthed more than he expected. It was more than enough. The earth gave him an abundance of grain, and in doing so, an abundance of wealth. Instead, of being filled with gratitude, he was filled with angst. What was he to do with it all?

*Then he said to himself, 'I will tear down my barns and build bigger ones, and there I will store **my** surplus grain. And **I'll** say to **myself**, "**You** have plenty of grain laid up for many years. Take life easy; eat, drink, and be merry."*

He would build more to house the extra. Yes, he thought. This will give me peace. I will give this gift to myself.

He would be king of his own palace. He would rid himself of this worry he felt and replace it with pleasure. This was the way—to discard what had already been given to make way for more. He would arrive with just a little more work, a little more time, a little more investment.

That very night, he died.[16]

Jesus tells the parable of the rich fool in Luke 12 in response to a demand from the crowd. A man shouted, "Tell my brother to divide the inheritance with me!"[17] After Jesus explains this is not His role, He says, "Watch out! Be on your guard against all kinds of greed; life does not consist in an abundance of possessions."[18]

The rich fool let his wealth own him. He was unable to see a life beyond himself. Theologian William Barclay writes, "There is no parable which is so full of the words *I, me, my* and *mine*. . . . The rich fool was aggressively self-centered."[19] The rich fool walked himself into a tunnel of more—focusing on securing a safe life, a comfortable life for himself. Instead of using the surplus to walk in the ways of God, he walked himself to the grave. And we all will "march to the grave empty-handed."[20] When life is going well, we can become hyper-vigilant in making sure it stays that way. Just like the rich fool, we can become greedy when life gives us much. Greed is born from fear. When we live in fear that the bottom could fall out of our abundance, we can save in excess. Not just monetarily, but also with time, resources, or by trying to avoid discomfort so much that we end up only half alive. Living purposefully requires risk. Following Jesus requires risk. If we live with a scarcity mindset, we can stop following Him without even realizing it. We can stop living lives that call us to get in the boat with Him even with the storm clouds above. We can stand on the shore, telling ourselves, *It is better here. This is the way. This is the way to peace. Right here, I will build up my house along the shore. I will keep myself secure. I will build up storage units in the back to hold the extra now. Then, then, I will follow Him once more.*

We can start playing it safe—too safe. A scarcity mindset can make us hoarders. Scarcity can also turn us inward too much, because out there, bad things might happen. Scarcity can keep us drawing within the lines because we convince ourselves that we will be safe within their confines. If we don't hope too much, dream too much, expect too much, then we won't fall too far. Jesus shows us how to be good change agents and good disrupters, even when it costs us. When we live in fear, we become greedy. We collect, protect, and hoard in more ways than one.

——— *&* ———

In *The Liturgy of Abundance, The Myth of Scarcity,* Walter Brueggemann argues that the Bible starts with abundance. Genesis 1 is a praise of God's lavish generosity. The Creator gives us good things and calls us very good too. There is such an abundance of goodness within creation that on the seventh day, God rested.[21] We see God's overflow of goodness pour out onto the people, the promise to Abraham that his descendants will be more than all the stars in the sky. Then the narrative shifts in Genesis 47, when Pharaoh, the leader of the Egyptian people, has a dream that there will be a famine in the land. It's the first time in the Bible where someone says there's not enough.[22] Pharaoh hires Joseph to manage this new economy of storing everything. When the Israelites run out of food, they come to Joseph with collateral. They give up their land and cattle for food until they have nothing left to give but themselves.

Scarcity mindset enslaves us. Having an abundant mindset—the mindset that says there is enough, the mindset that prompts us to share what we have, the mindset that helps us to climb out of the tunnel, to walk in the ways of Jesus—this is the way to freedom. This is not the kind of freedom the rich fool was looking for. It doesn't mean we can sit back and only focus on the security and pleasures of our own lives. Nor does it mean our lives will be safe. It means we find a life marked by love. Love is not always easy; love costs & a life marked by love is the only life worth living.

A 2023 study found that people with a scarcity mindset are less empathetic: Participants in the study who had a scarcity mentality rated the pain of others lower than did those who had an abundant mindset.[23] How can we love when we live as if there is not enough to go around? We can't.

An abundant mindset can help us to see connections, broaden our perspective, solve problems, and make decisions that will benefit us long-term, according to Kirkland.[24] So how do we develop an abundant mindset? One of her answers is the one we keep circling back to: gratitude. Gratitude helps us become aware of what we already have instead of fixating on what we don't have or on what we might lose. Gratitude helps us to stay present. Gratitude helps us avoid tunnel living.[25]

Brueggemann writes, "When people forget that Jesus is the bread of the world, they start eating junk food—the food of the Pharisees and of Herod, the bread of moralism and of power." Scarcity mentality is the primary ingredient in these junk foods.

When we believe the lie that God can't love us as we are, we become rigid. When we live as if others' wins are our own losses, we keep trying to dominate the playing field even though this life was never meant to be a competition. Scarcity mindset can get us so focused on rules that we begin to draw circles around those who don't follow suit. Scarcity mindset can have us desperately trying to elevate ourselves while diminishing others. Scarcity mindset prevents us living the full lives our abundant Creator desires for us.[26]

We cling to our power when we are afraid someone or something could take it away. So we build ourselves bigger barns to protect our wealth and we forget to take care of those around us. Or we live our lives in a way that has us avoiding things that can hurt us, desperately trying to grab all the power over our lives when we are only allotted a portion.

Like the Israelites of the Old Testament, we create and cling to idols when things are not going well. We're also guilty of clinging to idols when things *are* going well but we forget from whom all good things flow. We cling to idols when we fear this goodness could be ripped out from under us at any minute. Our idols are not carved out of wood or stone. Our idols are much like the rich fool's—the idea that our lives, our security, are all up to us. Like Pharaoh, we live out of a scarcity economy—one that says we have to protect ourselves no matter the cost. We can protect ourselves so much that it prevents us from living.

Jesus shows us a different kind of economy. In this economy, He creates more out of little. With leftover baskets of fish and bread, He is telling us something: He is enough. His ways feed us more than our algorithms, our financial investments, or our power ever can. The closer we stay to Jesus, the more we will live out of abundance. The closer we stay to Jesus, the more we will live.

&

As my friend and I wrapped up our conversation over my kitchen island, I told her a phrase I had recently learned: *That was before; this is now.*

An abundance mindset doesn't mean we ignore the lessons from our past hurts. An abundance mindset will not protect us from future hurts. We know that nothing is guaranteed. Disorder came for my friend and me more than once. One day, the dunes we are currently living on will shift again—for both of us. For all of us.

If you have the privilege of not knowing how fragile this life is, how fragile we are, the unexpected reveals it rather quickly. *&.* In the unknown there is another reality you can hold onto: You have a Creator who makes all things new. From year to year, from week to week, from day to day. Just because the worst-case scenario was part of your life for a time doesn't mean it will be this time. Even if what you fear becomes reality, God breathes new life into what is dead, with each changing season, after every storm, and in the promise of an empty grave. God can make new things bloom out of the darkness again and again.

As you sit with your humanity, with your real human fears that your good luck will run out, ground yourself in the present. Look up at the sky, look around your home and at the people who fill it; look out into the places where you are loved and where your love is needed, and let gratitude take over.

Breathe in—this is now.

Now is not perfect & now is so very good.

Help me to not let fear of tomorrow ruin the taste of abundance now.

& breathe out.

Life is not to be lived in tunnels. Life is not meant to be lived only half of the time. We co-create this life alongside the One who first breathed us into being. Whatever route we end up on, we have the choice to be present on it. We will feel scared at times & we get the choice to keep moving toward Jesus, toward abundance. This way is not the easy way. This way is not safe. This way is full of challenges & it is full of beauty.

In this life, there will be birth & death. There will be joy & trials. There will be success & there will be failure. There is no number of safety measures we can put in place that can prevent us from experiencing the fullness of what it means to be a human in these bodies that fail, with these souls that waver, and on this planet that aches. Instead of letting our human fragility terrify us, perhaps we can rest in this truth: We can only control so much. Thank God, it is not all up to us.

When we feel scared, when our negativity bias speaks louder than it ought, when we feel pulled to build up our kingdoms as a matter of protection, may we have the courage to be honest:

> I am scared this goodness will run out & I am grateful for the goodness of right now.
>
> I am scared there's not enough room for me & I am grateful my Creator says there is enough room for everyone.
>
> I am scared of making the wrong choice & I am grateful for a God who will hold me in the upswing or in the fallout.
>
> I am scared there won't be enough & I am grateful I have something to give.
>
> I am scared there isn't enough & I am grateful for all that I have.
>
> I am scared heartache will come & I know that if it does . . . God will somehow wrangle goodness out of it.

Because God is not scarce. He broke through heaven before to display His lavish love. He breaks through still. He breaks through the tunnels we create. He extends a hand and offers to guide us out. Because life was not meant to be lived underground, waiting to check off the next milestone, waiting to feel safer if we can just get to the next point. Life is meant to be lived with both feet on the ground, rooted in our difficult & good realities. Life is meant to be lived in this moment. These moments hold heartaches & beauty all at once. When we feel scared that goodness will run out, we point our faces toward the sun and in the truth the light shows us: Goodness may look different tomorrow than it does today, the darkness will eventually come, & the light will never disappear. The light will shine even in the darkness—today, tomorrow, evermore.

FURTHER READING

Psalm 27

❖ REFLECTION ❖

What are you scared about when life is relatively good? How does the line "Life is so beautiful & life can be so scary" resonate with you? How can you see a scarcity mindset played out in your past and present, thinking about times you felt insecure, jealous, greedy, or nervous? What would shifting to an abundant mindset (or more of an abundant mindset) look like for you?

& GRATITUDE PRACTICE

I'm scared about these things:

I find rest in knowing this:

I'm scared I'm not living up to:

I am grateful for a God who says this about me:

I feel scared that I'm not in control of:

I feel grateful for these constants in my life:

Part 2

DISORDER

||||||||||||||||||||||||||||||

I plead with a God of Maybe, who may or
may not let me collect more years. It is a
God I love, and a God that breaks my heart.

—Kate Bowler, *Everything Happens for
a Reason: And Other Lies I've Loved*

5

Grieving & Grateful

WE FINALLY SUMMONED the courage to try again. It was the spring of 2016, and we were living in Tucson, Arizona. We knew our days there were numbered. In a year, we would be packing up for the fourth time in four years and moving our lives to Texas for Andy's orthodontic residency. We were trying to soak in what we could of the West Coast on a limited budget. So we decided to pack our three-year-old daughter and eighteen-month-old son in our Toyota and drive sixteen hours to Yosemite National Park.

Although that did take a bit of bravery, the courage I'm referring to was the decision to begin trying for a third child. It took courage because the unexpected touched every part of our second pregnancy. It began with the pregnancy itself.

After trying for nearly a year for our first child, the second came by surprise. The unexpected continued with a bright spot on an ultrasound at twenty weeks that my doctor told me could be a sign of a trisomy, then bloodwork confirmed trisomy 21—also known as Down syndrome. The unexpected came again with a fetal echocardiogram that showed a hole in our son's heart. The unexpected was in the phone call my husband made to me, telling me that our request to move to a bigger city to care for our son was granted, though we would not be anywhere near family as we requested but instead further away. The unexpected flooded me the moment our son was born—the peace I had been praying for those twenty weeks arrived in the dim hospital room when our eyes met. The unexpected filled the phone line four months later: The cardiologist who had told me he was almost certain the hole in Anderson's heart would close on its own was wrong. Our son would need open-heart surgery. & the unexpected came once more in that hospital when, in what should have been the worst moments of my life, I had never felt God's presence more near. For four hours, we sat in the cardiac intensive care unit. Instead of feeling terror, I felt held.

This Disordered period had broken me apart. I was in the rebuilding process. Disorder had removed parts of me and left others. It was also adding new pieces that I was still trying to put together. Life was hard with my son with a disability. Doctor appointments were plentiful; therapies were too. I found myself isolated from people I once knew. I was often on the outside looking in with new friend groups who could not know my reality, who could not know the unbecoming and becoming that takes place after life is upended. They could not speak my new language of disability and medical acronyms. They could not know my fears. They could know me, but not fully. I was getting to know me all over again.

My identity was shifting alongside my hard & beautiful life with my son. I was changing and I was transforming. I was seeing the beauty in it. I was beginning to notice things I had turned my face away from before. I was seeing in different shades, colors I had never known. It's as if I was reborn the day my son entered the world and I was learning how to live all over again. I was fresh, and tender, and scared. I knew the truth: No one is immune to life. Although I was grateful—so grateful for my son, so grateful for all he was teaching me, in all the ways God was transforming me through him—that did not mean I wanted to go through the unexpected again. I had lived enough to know that the more we open our hearts up to love, the more vulnerable they become to breaking.

Nearly a year after Anderson's open-heart surgery, we made our way to Yosemite. We had a picnic at the base of Yosemite's El Capitan. Violet played in a stream, and Anderson happily took pieces of bread and cheese with his small, pudgy hands. Andy and I poured a glass of wine and took in the iconic scene. Our lives were unrecognizable in the three years since becoming parents & our lives were quite gorgeous like the sight in front of us. There was room left on the picnic blanket. Our hearts still had room to grow.

El Capitan "started forming about 220 million years ago when the North American tectonic plate collided with the neighboring plate under the ocean. This forced the Pacific Plate beneath what is now California."[1] The magma that was pushed to the surface crystallized into granite, and eventually, "erosion carved El Capitan from the Sierra Nevada."[2] During the last Ice Age, glaciers carved out the valley floor for the final appearance of the three thousand vertical feet of sheer granite. El Capitan is the largest piece of granite in the world, attracting thousands to take in its views every year. It is the product of destruction & the transformation that can come after. It is still evolving by the forces of nature that change its shape ever so slowly. Granite is a very strong, durable rock—and even it is not immune to change. The rock has been through much and it is not done being formed. We are never done being formed. As long as our lungs take in air, we will be shaped by life.

Andy and I had been torn down to the studs through Disorder, and something beautiful was being created from the erosion. We decided to open ourselves up to possible destruction once more—knowing there were no guarantees. Knowing that beauty would be present somehow, no matter the outcome.

Then it happened. Several months later, we were at my in-laws' house in Georgia. It was time to take another pregnancy test. Andy and I waited for a few seconds, and there it was—a second pink line. Andy said, "We're going to be outnumbered," with a huge grin on his face. We cried. We told my in-laws because they would notice my not drinking champagne at my brother-in-law and soon-to-be sister-in-law's wedding the next day. We danced that night away, knowing how fragile new love makes you, and yet trying to believe good things were to come. This would be the afterglow, we told ourselves as we swayed to the beat. We had to.

The wedding festivities ended, and we landed back home. I had morning sickness, and then commented to a friend that it was much lighter than during my first two pregnancies. I had an uneasy feeling bubbling below the surface as I continued living normal life. On our trips to the grocery store, when I put the kids down for naps, and at our many regularly scheduled appointments, there it was, brewing, alerting me that something was happening. I walked into one of those weekly therapy appointments for Anderson, and the bubbling became a roaring boil. I felt tears, produced by fear and a knowing, start to well up. I had to excuse myself and let the therapists take over his session. I slid down to the bathroom tiles in the pediatric therapy clinic and verbally pleaded, "God, don't do this to me again, don't do this to me again, don't do this to me again." I didn't know what I was praying for exactly. I just knew something was wrong and didn't want it to be so. I wanted it to be my imagination, not my reality. A week later, my reality came in small drops of blood. I googled. It was light. Google told me it was probably fine. I booked an appointment and hoped. My mind played tug-of-war between terror and telling myself it was the past trauma speaking. *It's over. No, after all we have been through, we are due for a break.*

But hearts that have been broken are not immune from being broken again.

At the appointment, we saw on the big screen a pea-sized baby with no heartbeat. Exactly two years earlier, we'd had an ultrasound and found out our unborn son had possible genetic conditions and heart defects. There we were again, another ultrasound, another round of heartache. Only this time, no heartbeat.

We would check again in a week; perhaps my pregnancy was in an earlier stage than I thought, they told me. But it wasn't. I knew it wasn't. We went back, and again, nothing. The baby was smaller than the week before. It turns out that the baby had stopped growing the day before my bathroom-floor meltdown. It was happening again. The darkness covered me. The tunnel started forming. How, how could we be facing heartache again so soon? How could it be over? How was I on another ultrasound bed with tears running down my face? Hadn't I learned enough? Hadn't I been through enough? How was I supposed to keep going?

I wonder if that has happened to you? The moments after getting gut-wrenching news make everything become hyper-focused. You are aware of your news and unable to process how the news can be real. You are unable to process how the world is still moving along and yet somehow you must. You still have to schedule the appointment at the front desk and move one foot in front of the other to your car. You don't know if you are to cry or to sit there wrapped in numbness. You don't know how to keep going, and yet your lungs still take in air. It feels harsh that life still moves on when yours falls apart & it is these moments that are marked by Grace. In these moments we are aware of how God makes us fragile & also resilient. We are built to keep going, to keep evolving. Like the granite of El Capitan, we are strong and yet malleable. We evolve even when we don't want to. Like the rocks, we cannot control the external forces that cut into us. Unlike the rocks, we get to decide what shape we will now take on.

———— *&* ————

In this section, we will explore gratitude when we enter Disordered periods. How do we stay present to the light when all feels dark? Grief is a gateway to deeper understanding. So too is gratitude. Gratitude is not the solution to pain. Rather, the two are deeply intertwined. Author and mindfulness teacher Oren Jay Sofer puts it this way, "Gratitude and grief may seem to be in tension with one another, but gratitude and loss are inseparable. Awareness of what is present calls forth what is absent. Grief embodies our humanity even as gratitude allows us to embrace pain and hardship."[3]

Grief & gratitude can open us up to the whole of life, the whole of who we are, and can usher us into who we hope to become. This doesn't mean we count the loss as good. It means this: To live is to lose, and we can't lose anything without having loved it first. In this life, we will love *&* we will lose. We will grieve *&* we will be thankful for the good things we once had, the good things we still carry with us, and the good things we have not yet known but believe Love is drawing us toward.

Everything I include in this section of the book can be considered under the umbrella of grieving, as we experience all sorts of emotions when grieving. In this chapter I focus on the initial emotional state of getting knocked down by life, whether this event was unexpected or was something you saw coming but could not prepare for what the fallout would feel like. We will start at the moment of loss—and loss can take many forms. I wonder what loss looks like or looked like for you? Have you lost someone you love or someone you didn't get the chance to love fully? Have you lost a relationship you thought was forever? Maybe your loss has come because you realized you had to walk away from someone or some entity that hurt you too many times. Maybe you lost your religion or the community that once held you. In a society averse to grief, there is another loss we might experience alongside our other losses: We can lose the belonging we once knew before grief compelled us to be more honest about life's darker parts.

"Experts have a pretty good sense of the path that grief takes through the mind," according to *New York Times* writer Ann Finkbeiner. First is a state of shock, in which we feel numb or sad, angry, guilty, anxious, scatterbrained, or unable to sleep or eat—or any combination of the above. During those first weeks, the grieving "have increased heart rates, higher blood pressure and may be more likely to have heart attacks."[4]

Author and psychotherapist Francis Weller writes that grief comes in many forms and is "a visitor to be welcomed, not shunned."[5] When grief is not expressed, "it tends to harden the once-vibrant parts of us," as Weller puts it.[6] However, he argues that grief is not a permanent address where we take up residence, but rather "a companion that walks beside us," summarizing,

> The work of the mature person is to carry grief in one hand and gratitude in the other and to be stretched large by them. How much sorrow can I hold? That's how much gratitude I can give. If I carry only grief, I'll bend toward cynicism and despair. If I have only gratitude, I'll become saccharine and won't develop much compassion for other people's suffering. Grief keeps the heart fluid and soft, which helps make compassion possible.[7]

To become compassionate toward ourselves and one another, we walk with grief honestly and resist hiding it the way our culture may tell us to & we can do so without losing sight of the light, even if it is a distant flicker. The premise of my first book, *The Gift of the Unexpected*, is that we have to undergo the unexpected if we ever hope to be transformed by it. Experiencing our Disordered periods means going all the way through the pain. Grief is worthy of our time. Jesus rose, yes. But not without first grieving, not without dying.

———— & ————

He knew what was coming. Everyone must die, but few know how they will die. Even fewer know the hour. He knew. He had been warning His followers that His time was near the end. They didn't want to believe Him. Perhaps they wanted to believe He was speaking to them in hyperbole, as He so often did. *Perhaps they wanted to believe He was speaking to them in stories with a hidden meaning, He often did that too. But there was no hidden meaning. There was no exaggeration. Death was coming. The most painful death created by people, His beloved, was coming for Him.*

He sat down and broke bread with His closest friends and one who would hand Him over to be tortured. He spoke parting words, He told them about His love and how they were meant to carry it forward. They didn't know He was giving a eulogy.

He went to the Garden of Gethsemane to pray with His closest three friends. He said to them, "My soul is overwhelmed with sorrow to the point of death."[8] *His mind, body, and heart were heavy with despair. He prayed, "My Father, if it is possible, may this cup be taken from me. Yet not as I will, but as you will."*[9] *He wanted to show the world the depth of God's unending love. He just wanted a different path to get there. Who wouldn't? He prayed this prayer again, and once more.*

But the cup was not taken away. He would have to drink the bitter wine that would lead to the most excruciating six hours.[10]

I used to be only a resurrection person. I used to want to skip over the messiness of Holy Week—the betrayal, the trial, the torture. Especially the torture. I wanted the good news. I was a resurrection person before I had experienced the depth of what it means to be human. I was a resurrection person before I had experienced heartache and what felt like forsakenness. Before the unexpected, I wanted tidy. But resurrection is messy. Jesus' final days on earth were brutal & this is now where I see the good news.

Death by crucifixion was developed by the Persians in 300–400 BC and was "perfected by the Romans" in 100 BC; it might be the most painful method of torture ever developed and it is where the word *excruciating* comes from.[11] Before Jesus was crucified, Pilate ordered Him to be flogged. The whip would have been composed of leather with metal balls in the middle and sheep bones at the end. The metal would have caused deep bruising, and the sheep bones would have torn out chunks of flesh and exposed Jesus' bone beneath.[12] When the flogging was finished and the Romans placed a crown of thorns on his head to mock him, the thorns would have caused more bleeding and nerve damage, intensifying the pain in Jesus' neck and face.[13] The Romans nailed his wrists and feet with seven-inch spikes, which would have severed the median nerve, causing intense pain and paralysis of the hands. In only a few minutes, His shoulders, and then arms and wrists would be dislocated. The weight of His hanging body would force Him to bear his weight on his chest. He had to force Himself to breathe as the weight caused the rib cage to lift in a nearly constant state of inhalation.[14]

For six hours, on a horrific & Good Friday, Jesus showed us unrelenting solidarity. The good news is rooted in the darkness where God chose to join us and chooses to meet us still. The good news is that Jesus took on every piece of humanity. With death He could have stopped, but He instead chose to pursue us to the bitter end. He took on the darkest of darks this life has to offer. The good news is that the darkness is not where Jesus' story ended. The good news is our story won't end there either.

As we walk through the painful parts of our lives, we move forward knowing new life will one day come. Resurrection is not just a promise of the life after. It is available to us here and now. The little deaths we experience in this life are to be redeemed. Not necessarily with tidy endings, but eventually, where God fills in the dark spaces and breathes in new beginnings.

I am still a resurrection person—it's just that now I realize I am also Good Friday person. I no longer want to skip over the hard parts of Holy Week. We can't skip over the hard parts of our own lives, nor should we. Instead, we carry them with us and trust in God's grace to help us move forward and to move forward differently than we once did.

When we can't see the light, may we go back to the garden where Jesus once stood. May we be honest as He was honest. May we admit to ourselves, may we admit to Him, that our souls are overwhelmed with sorrow. May we admit we are on the brink of despair. May we let ourselves descend deeper into the darkness. *&*. As we go further down into our grief, may we know there is not a level of darkness God does not intimately know. He was torn apart, mocked, stripped of the very air in His lungs so that we would know we are not alone. There is no depth we can sink to where God has not already been.

We do not have to be thankful for the darkness *&* we can be thankful for the God who intimately knows its power. I hope we can be thankful for a God who did not shy away from His pain *&* yet in His final moments found a way to pull us into His unending goodness. This goodness is the way of love and it flows and flows, even in our darkest moments, ushering us to the light once more.

———— & ————

I went home from the hospital with an empty body and a once again fractured heart. A week later, I had to go to a Down syndrome conference in Texas for an organization I was a part of. Because of my online presence, the women there knew about my loss and met me with grace. These were women who had known the unexpected in one way or another. They shared their own stories of miscarriage with me. They gave me knowing looks. They met me with kindness.

They knew the part of me that felt like we deserved an uneventful pregnancy after all we had been through with our son. They knew the part of me that felt ashamed over my grief, as 10 to 20 percent of pregnancies end in miscarriage.[15] They also reminded me that if we feel as though we are not entitled to our pain or that we can't talk about it because others experience far greater pain, we would all hurt silently. We are all subjected to and connected by the joys and sorrows of the human experience.

On the flight back to Arizona, back to reality, I had to put my book down because I could not be distracted from my grief. This was a part of my story I could not make sense of, and I never would. No new potential baby would replace this baby. I looked out the airplane window, and even through teary eyes, the sight looked familiar: white sands with dots of dark green juniper bushes. I pulled up the screen on the back of the seat in front of me. We were flying over Alamogordo, New Mexico—the site of my before-and-after moment. We lived in Alamogordo when we learned our lives would never be the same. It was where we learned our son had Down syndrome. It was the place where I thought my life was ending, and in some ways, it did. It was the end of my old ways of being, my old ways of believing. Looking at that part of New Mexico now with a bird's-eye view, I also knew it was a beginning. There in the New Mexican desert was the beginning of a new life, the beginning of a new me.

As I headed over that old desert and into the new one we now lived in, I was reminded that the desert is dry with unrelenting heat, yes & the desert is the source of unique life. The desert produces striking things that simply can't grow elsewhere. My heart had been broken more than once in the desert. It was broken now. I could feel the pain as acutely as if I had run my hands over the sharp cactus spines in my backyard & I was grateful for how this jagged landscape was continuing to bring new life out of me. Despite the mounting sand piles and thorny shrubs, my heart was finding a way to blossom here. Maybe even because of them. No, there would be no solution, no neat bow to put on this part of my story. The only good things to come out of this loss would be a continuing change from within. If our grief makes us more compassionate, compassion still had room to grow in me. I was in the thick of the desert heat once more & I knew I was not done blooming. I wiped tears from my eyes as the truth poured over me: We are never through. Everything that happens to us may not be good; this was not good & yet good things had grown from this dry ground before. As we flew out of the Chihuahua Desert of my past and into the Sonoran Desert of my present, I was reminded of all God had already grown in me. Good things would grow again. They were already growing. Something new was coming. I could feel it.

The Garden at Gethsemane sits on the lower slopes of the Mount of Olives, which is just outside the Judean desert. Gethsemane in Hebrew is *gat shemanim*—which means oil press. This suggests the garden was a grove of olive trees where an oil press was located.[16] This garden was meant to grow something, which would then be crushed and pressed to make something new with each sprout. It was this garden that held the tears of a God who would be crushed and pressed and made new.

Disorder is like this for us too. Disorder crushes us, presses us, and in the end, with the care of the grower, we become something different than what we once started as. May we walk through the desert knowing our grief is worthy & we are not alone in it. May we sit on the dry ground feeling the weight of love lost & may we know we are loved still. May we sit with our grief long enough that we are able to walk to new ground. When we get there, may we run our hands along the olive trees & know that in the crushing and pressing, Jesus was made new. May we ask Him to make something new out of us. When our circumstances are nothing to be grateful for, may we hold on to the One who intimately knows the depth of our pain. & if His solidarity is the only thing we can bear to be grateful for, may we pray it be enough.

When I came home from the conference, I knew we had to honor this child's life. Genetic testing showed us she was a girl. Andy and I lay atop our bed with pen and paper. We cried as we made a list of names for a daughter we would never hold. I wondered, *How do we keep doing this?* How do we keep trying in a world with no guarantees that pain won't once again rip through our home? I wondered if we would ever make our way out of the desert.

We remembered that a life lived in the shadows of comfort is no life at all. We could not allow fear to rule our hearts; love would. As we lay there tangled in each other's grief & the glow of our love for each other, we knew we would keep going. We did not know what would come next, yet there was a hope that was somehow still beating. We finished the list of names, and my husband picked one of them immediately. We took in deep, staggered breaths as we held hands, hands that had held each other's tears for two years in exam rooms, in surgery waiting rooms, and in the quiet of our bedroom.

Before we turned out the lights, I went to bed believing that the God who wept in the Garden was with our daughter. Because of this God, we have a daughter we will one day meet.

FURTHER READING
Psalm 77

❖ REFLECTION ❖

Name your most recent loss. Consider whether the grief you carry is an enduring expression of love. Ask yourself how you can carry grief over the loss in one hand & gratitude in the other. Jesus asked for His fate to be changed three times. How does His sorrow and expression of humanity make you feel about your own sorrow and your own desire for change?

& GRATITUDE PRACTICE

My heart is/was full of sorrow over this:

I can/could see the light peeking through the darkness in this way:

I feel disappointed in God's involvement or what feels like a lack of involvement in my loss in this way:

I feel comforted He knows suffering because:

I'm tired of my time in the desert because I'm tired of feeling this way:

I'm grateful the desert has bloomed / is blooming these new things in me:

6

Angry & Grateful

As soon as the doctor told us it was safe to try again, we did. My brother-in-law and sister-in-law called to announce their first baby was on the way shortly afterward. They were due in July. We were happy for them, congratulated them, and in my gut, I knew I was pregnant too. After a weird dizzy spell, I took a test earlier than recommended, and I was right—positive.

Instead of feeling scared after the miscarriage, I had this calm assurance that everything was fine this time. Sometimes, we tell ourselves we will be okay because it is the only way we can keep going. I had two ultrasounds and bloodwork done at ten weeks that showed no genetic anomalies. We were having a boy! All signs looked good, so we told our family, friends, and Violet and Anderson at thirteen weeks.

Two days later, the goodness, the confidence, and the peace I had around this pregnancy fell apart when a nurse tried to find a heartbeat with a doppler and couldn't. We locked eyes. She could feel my own heart start beating at a rapid pace. Andy wasn't with me. I had told him to go to work because a fourteen-week appointment is pretty uneventful. Now, it was a full-scale event, the type of event I had played the main character in before. I was tired of being cast in this recurring role.

The nurse walked me back to an ultrasound room. The hallway closed in around me. The ultrasound technician took out her wand and immediately found the baby and his heartbeat. Relief. But this was my third baby. The black-and-white images on the nearly movie-theater-sized screen didn't look right. She quickly sent me to a room. I had been in this room before. It's the room at the ob-gyn's office where they give you news you don't want to hear. It's the room of the unexpected. It's sometimes the room of death. I paced and paced as I waited. Another nurse walked in and took me back to the ultrasound room one more time. This time, the images were clear. The baby's stomach was bigger than his head.

The doctor finally came in and explained it was likely a fluid-filled cyst and could indicate several issues. He told me to come back in two weeks. And then life kept moving—as it always does. I called my mom first. I explained to her in very matter-of-fact detail that something was wrong. Again. I told her this while parked outside my children's preschool. It was the same preschool that, less than a year prior, I had left and gotten a call from Anderson's cardiologist informing me that he would need open-heart surgery. Then I called Andy on his lunch break. I don't remember his response. I just remember how we felt—how did we keep ending up here? I forced a smile as I walked across the school courtyard. My body was present. My soul was somewhere else. Disconnected. Numb. Shocked. We got home, and I swiped peanut butter on bread. I put *Bubble Guppies* on the TV. I wiped down the kids' sticky faces and then tucked them in for nap time.

Then the fire ignited.

I cried, I pleaded. I had never prayed for one of my children as much as I had already prayed over this new son. I prayed he would be gentle, yet strong, a defender of his brother, a friend to his sister, and a man of integrity.

And here I was. In the same house. In the same desert. Praying once more. Only this time, praying that he survived.

I thought this was the rainbow after the storm, but it wasn't. It was a different kind of storm—a firestorm. I wondered how many times a person could break before the pieces were so chiseled down they couldn't be put back together again.

Here I was—breaking again.

The falling pieces were flammable.

The flames grew quickly.

Where was this God who promised to never leave, never forsake?

Where was this God who knits us together in the womb?

Where was this God who gives life to the full?

Not in my house.

I felt God had forgotten me.

This great Savior did not save me from the flames.

So I let it burn.

&

The largest wildfire in American history burned in 1910. Three million acres went up in smoke in the Northern

Rockies, killing seventy-eight people. After the fire, the United States Forest Service established policies to put out all fires. Fifteen years later, in 1935, the 10 A.M. Policy went into effect, "dictating that fires must be contained and controlled by 10 o'clock the morning after their initial report."[1] The 10 A.M. Policy emphasized fire suppression for decades until, toward the middle of the twentieth century, research began revealing something unexpected: Fire is a natural and necessary process for the healthy growth of forests.[2]

Fires occur naturally through lightning strikes, spontaneous combustion of decaying organic matter, and through the sun's heat, for example.[3] Forest fires are needed because they clear the woods of the accumulated decaying organic matter on the forest floor that fuels wildfires. Without occasional fires to clear this away, a fire may grow, moving more quickly and doing more damage than a controlled burn.[4] When fires are allowed to clear the underbrush of the forest, more sunlight reaches the soil, nourishing it, which allows trees to grow stronger, and fires also kill insects and diseases that prey on trees.[5]

Some trees have fire-resistant bark and cones that require heat-release seeds for regeneration. The same goes for certain species of plants that encourage fire by having flammable resins. Without fire, these trees and plants would die with no new generations to carry on.[6] Even some animals depend on fire. The sole food source for the endangered Karner Blue Butterfly caterpillar is wild lupine. Wild lupine requires fire to maintain an ecosystem balance in which it can thrive. Without fire, the lupines can't grow, and the caterpillars cannot consume enough food to undergo metamorphosis and become butterflies.[7]

We have to let fires burn to let the sun in. We have to let fires burn to survive. We have to let fires burn for new life to be born. Flames are required for transformation. Otherwise, like the caterpillars, we die in the same form we've always known. If we don't let fires burn, we die without ever getting the chance to fully live. Fire can cause death & fire can give life.

In 1978, the U.S. Forest Service got rid of its 10 A.M. Policy and shifted from a strategy of fire suppression to fire management. However, the suppression strategies are still having effects on the forests today, including a fuel buildup that means today's wildfires are larger and harder to control than they would have been if the fuel sources had been allowed to burn off naturally.[8] Not letting fires burn has consequences. Not letting fires burn results in bigger, more damaging, and more deadly fires.

So too it is with us.

---------- & ----------

Psalm 13 is a complaint Psalm. Complaint Psalms make up a large portion of the Psalms of Disorientation.

Brueggemann writes, "These psalms are the voices of those who find their circumstance dangerously, and not just inconveniently, changed. And they do not like it. . . . It is the function of these songs to enable, require, and legitimate the complete rejection of the old orientation. That old arrangement is seen, if not as fraud, at least as inadequate to the new circumstance."[9]

Part of my anger stemmed from wanting to walk away from God but being unable to do so. My beliefs about biblical interpretation are malleable. I hold my worldview with open hands, willing to adapt as I grow, learn new things, and unlearn others. However, I couldn't get over the God who came to suffer with us. I can't. He is too compelling. I was left to make sense of a God who sometimes intervenes and sometimes does not. I was left to make sense of a God who had said no to many tearful requests. I was left with a God who was different than the God I had hoped for. The fire was making a way for me to discover this God in light of the flames.

Psalm 13, a psalm of David, begins, "How long, LORD? Will you forget me forever?"

David asks three more times in vv. 1–2, "How long . . . how long . . . how long?"

We ask "How long?" when we are standing on the outside of what used to make sense. We ask "How long?" when we are wondering not only about God's timing but also about God's integrity.[10] David wonders how God can neglect him in his time of need. David seems confused, anxious, and angry as he prepares to face his enemies alone.

I wonder what it is you are facing or have faced that has left you asking the same question. I wonder if someone you love is lying upon a hospital bed for days now, and they are left—you are left—in that in-between space asking, *Is God even here?* I wonder if you have lost a love and are ready for new love to enter your life; you have been waiting and waiting and ask, *Will it ever be my turn again?* I wonder if you have an illness that pains you, that makes every day difficult, that makes some days unbearable, and have questioned, *Is God still good?*

If I were sitting across from you right now, I would look into your tired eyes. The last thing I would do is point out what is still good. The last thing I would do is "at least" you or "bright side" you. Instead, I would tell you to let it burn. Let the fire rage. The fire may not have happened for a purpose, but purpose can come from it. That purpose can be a clearing, a clearing of the decaying matter on the floor of your soul. This fire can also make a way for a new clarity, a new path, for new life to grow.

Psalm 13 does not end the way it begins. It begins with David crying out to God, then he demands more: "Look on me and answer, LORD my God" (v. 3). David feels that God is ignoring his plight—ignoring *him*. David needs to be seen. In the same verse, he pleads, "Give light to my eyes or I will sleep in death." He's asking for hope. He's asking for signs of life within the flames. Then, something changes. After the plea for deliverance. After expressing his deepest frustrations, disappointments, and anger, David ends the psalm this way: "But I trust in your unfailing love; my heart rejoices in your salvation. I will sing the LORD's praise, for He has been good to me."

First, anger, then gratitude. The Psalm begins with questions, with fury and demands, and then turns into praise. Anger, lament, is a pathway to see God again, perhaps in a way we have not experienced before. The fire can help us see Grace that was there before the fire ever sparked, maybe in ways our hearts could not even recognize before we were touched by the flames. Love was there before, Love is present during, and Love will continue after the fire burns out.

---------- *&* ----------

Two weeks after the ultrasound that showed our son's abdomen filled with fluid, we went back for another look. The fluid looked different this time, but it was still there. The doctor told us images indicated something was severely wrong, possibly deadly. We knew if this unknown diagnosis was something that could be helped by fetal intervention surgery, we had to have an amniocentesis. So, for the second time in two years, I agreed to one. The doctor took the needle out and injected it into my abdomen, and I couldn't stop the tears.

I've been through this before, so why does this hurt so much this time? Am I doing the right thing? What if he's already weak and I'm putting him at more risk? God, where are you?

I wailed on the table. I was unable to hide the pain from my husband. I felt so betrayed. Why would God allow us to walk down the road of another agonizing pregnancy? I was fanning the flames. I needed to. How could we be here again? I had no explanation. I had no answers. I felt empty. Abandoned. Confused. And then we went home to wait.

When I couldn't feel the heat, I felt nothing. I plastered a pleasant smile on my face. I forced giggles when playing with my kids. I waited for a call one Friday for the amniocentesis results that never came. We could go the weekend without staring at our phones. Then it was Monday.

Heavy chest. Inhale, exhale. Stare at the wall. Clean the house. Lie down. More staring. Breathing was difficult. No phone call again. The results must be bad. Or maybe not. No answers, more waiting. How long, Lord?

Finally, a call. A clear report. A small dose of relief. Then, we went in for our eighteen-week anatomy scan. The ultrasound tech placed the warm gel on my still-small belly. *Deep breaths in, the squeeze of my husband's hand, and our boy up on the big screen.* The tech gently took us through everything she saw. She was trying to be encouraging, but the fluid in his abdomen was still there, and now there was fluid around his heart.

She showed us his bladder and pointed out the keyhole shape of it. *Okay*, we thought, *it must be posterior urethral valves.* PUV is a blockage in the urethra that can cause kidney damage and prevent proper lung development. It was one of the theories the doctor from the week prior had brought up. This week, the bladder was not only a different shape, but it also had a hole in it. *Oh no—something else is wrong.*

The technician finished her hour-long picture session and walked out of the room. My husband and I sat in silence, waiting for the new doctor, who we were sure was about to bring us more bad news. The doctor made some small talk with us as she tried to feel us out about where we were with keeping the pregnancy. She then confirmed our son did have PUVs. Then she started talking about his kidneys. She must have been going off of the previous week's reports because she started talking about bright spots. That's when the ultrasound technician spoke up with, "I didn't see that." The doctor reviewed the images, and her solemn attitude started changing. She didn't see any signs this time that indicated kidney damage. The ultrasound technician then prompted her to look at the bladder.

She confirmed the hole and said, "I don't know if you're praying people, but this hole in his bladder may be an answered prayer." The broken bladder was relieving pressure, protecting his kidneys, and allowing his lungs to develop.

Of course I had prayed in the four weeks leading up to this scan. I prayed angrily. I believed God could take this away from us. Every prayer was returned with the worst ultrasound from the week before. Why would today be any different? In my pain and pride, I started to doubt God's goodness to me. I knew God was good, but between a life-altering genetic diagnosis, open-heart surgery, a miscarriage, and now this—was God good *to me?*

A broken bladder was somehow a blessed miracle. We were not out of the fire, as there were still issues to tackle and medical plans to draw up, but God calmed the flames. I could see the forest on the other side of the smoke. More life would unfold. It was unfolding.

———————— *&* ————————

Notre Dame de Paris is the most famous Gothic cathedral of the Middle Ages. It's known for its many relics, including the crown of thorns Jesus was said to have worn on the day of His crucifixion. Notre Dame was also famed for its intricate stained-glass windows and the 314-foot spire, which was an architectural feat of its time.[11] On April 15, 2019, the cathedral burned. The fire was likely caused by either a cigarette or an electrical issue.[12] The flames took much of the 850-year-old church that more than 12 million people visit each year.[13] The fire ripped through the attic, melted the roof's lead sheath, and endangered the entire building. The spire that had graced the Parisian skyline for centuries came crashing down, punching giant holes into vaults and sending sheets of molten metal and charred beams falling below. Onlookers watched helplessly, horrified that this constant, this beautiful piece of living history, was going up in smoke.

The fire was not completely extinguished until the following day. I remember watching the news, in awe that amid the charred beams and twisted metal, the large golden altar cross still stood. The lit votives, each one representing someone's prayer, still burned.[14] Jesus does not leave us in the fire. He still hears our prayers as the fire closes in on us. Nothing can separate us from God. Not even the flames.

The reconstruction of Notre Dame began in 2019. Hundreds of people began putting the iconic landmark back together.[15] Even though the spire once again scrapes the sky, even though the debris is swept away, and even though its appearance on the outside looks much like the cathedral we once knew, it is not the same. The fire took away parts of

Notre Dame that will never come back. We are changed by the fires that burn us.

I would change once again from this new set of flames. I would not be a person who tells you, "It will all work out." I knew. I now knew that some people experience more life than others. It would give me eyes to see those people. It would give me eyes to see myself. This fire would shape me once again, in ways that I didn't know I needed to be reformed & it would burn me. We can't downplay trauma. This fire would be devastating.

And yet, the cross still stood.

It still stands.

My views of God, myself, this life were not the same as they were before the fire. The view that God is behind every detail of our lives melted in the heat. The view that God's justice meant God will right all the wrongs burnt to ashes. The view that we can earn our way to security if only we try hard enough went up in smoke.

The fire burned up the clutter and allowed me to see some things more clearly—closer to what they are, as they had always been. Anger can strip the land of our lives of unnecessary brush. Anger cannot change our circumstances & anger can help us to see life more clearly: Life is amazingly beautiful & at times purely devastating. God is somehow present at this intersection.

This pregnancy was not fair & one day I would look back and see God at work in it.

I had been through too much in too short a time & one day I would be able to see how God shaped me through it.

I didn't know that by letting my anger burn, I was not walking farther away from God. Instead, I was drawing closer to the God we have.

If you need to scream at God, raise your voice.

If you need to wail at the unfairness of life, let your tears fall.

If you are asking "How long?" with no answer, know that you are not the only one asking. Know that you will not be the last. Know that we are all connected by this question that none of us have the power to answer.

&

When the flames start to calm just a bit, we look at the ground where our feet still stand. We look at what is dead & what is not. We mourn the good things that have been lost & we keep our eyes open for new life that will one day come. Because it will come.

Then we look ahead, over the tops of the flames. The land will look different from what we once knew. We look forward and know that, in one way or another, we will one day leave this burnt earth. We will be marked by loss as we move forward & we can carry this loss to new life. We may not get rescued, we may always carry marks of the fire, & we move forward knowing goodness will come again. Even if that goodness looks different from what we once imagined. Because God stands inside the flames and also outside. God is behind us, with us, and in front of us. This God draws us into the future, one where we will be scarred from the burns & one where God makes new life sprout along a path we never envisioned being on or one we simply did not want to take.

Maybe the flames are too bright right now. Maybe the smoke is too thick. Know this: The flames cannot last forever.

I focused this chapter around my anger toward God. But you should know that as I was writing it, I was coming off a long period of anger toward another. I believed our relationship was one way, and really it had always been another. I just couldn't see it. So I kept trying, trying, trying to make it the way I wanted it to be, the way I thought it should be. One day, a spark turned into a flame and the flame turned into wildfire. My anger burned down what needed to die. After letting it burn for months, I could see. I could not change the circumstance and I would not change this person. Yet, the fire helped me to see the relationship for what it actually was. With time, I realized I did not want to build a home on the scorched land. I left the ashes behind, turned around, and walked in a different direction. This is possible for you too.

Anger is not good & yet it can be. Anger is not bad & yet it can be. Once the fire dies, we do our best to not start another with the ashes left behind. Instead, we notice how the smoke that once clouded our vision has somehow made our sight clearer than it was before. We can see—that we are not protected from it all & we are protected from much. God gives beauty for ashes.[16] May we have eyes to see it and a heart to be thankful for it. Maybe one day you will find yourself standing on scorched ground with new blooms around your feet. Maybe you will one day say God is good. & even, God is good to me.

FURTHER READING

Psalm 13

❖ REFLECTION ❖

What were you taught about anger? Think about whether your anger has been affirmed and whether people in your life tried/try to suppress your anger. Do you consider Jesus a friend? How does this answer affect how you express or suppress your anger with Him?

& GRATITUDE PRACTICE

I am/have been angry at God over this:

I feel hopeful God will make new life come out of the flames in this way / I feel grateful that God has brought new life out of the flames in this way:

I feel angry I will never get this back that burned in the flames:

I am seeing beauty in how I have changed / am changing because of the flames:

I am angry that God is not who I thought God to be in this way:

I am grateful for the God I actually have in this way:

7

Crying & Grateful

SPRING/SUMMER 2017
SAN ANTONIO, TEXAS/HOUSTON, TEXAS

DURING OUR MILITARY YEARS, every time we had to move, I was pregnant or had just given birth. Even in our final move, to where we are now in Florida, I was up against a tight deadline for my first book baby. But in 2017, it was a real live, struggling baby growing inside me.

Moving for any family is stressful. Add in a child with a significant disability and a high-risk pregnancy, and it is even more so. The amount of coordinating Andy and I had to do for medical care before our May departure date, on top of all the normal moving logistics, was overwhelming. Somehow, once again, we did it. We did it together. We said goodbye to Arizona, the state that held our many endings and beginnings, a state that held the best friends and witnesses to our unbecoming and becoming, but she would not see the conclusion of this ongoing. The outcome was yet to be determined, but the destination where it would unfold was set. I cried sad & grateful tears as we left the desert in the rearview. We were headed to San Antonio, Texas, for Andy to start his orthodontic residency.

We did the normal move-in things. We slept in a military hotel and then ate takeout on lawn chairs inside a barren house. We collapsed at the end of move-in day and were thankful we remembered to pack clean towels in our suitcases. We lived in a makeshift setup for the first couple of days while Andy went to work and began checking off the tedious in-processing list. About a week after we moved in, Andy was still in-processing when his new bosses asked him how my pregnancy was going. Instead of giving them the generic answer they were probably expecting, he told them the truth.

After the first few move-in days, we met with the fetal intervention team at Texas Children's Hospital in Houston—three and a half hours away from our new house in San Antonio. It was Andy's thirtieth birthday. Instead of clinking glasses, we were holding hands in waiting rooms between meetings with a maternal fetal specialist, pediatric urologist, pediatric nephrologist, pediatric orthopedic surgeon (this baby also had clubbed feet), and the worst of it was an hour-long MRI. I lay there in that tube, on my side, with the rhythmic and blaring wom, wom, wom. I had a technician pipe in music from MercyMe. A song about how even if God does not come to the rescue, faith will not waver. Tears trickled from my eyes and onto my temples as I heard the music and the machine. I was spent. I was surrendered because what else could I be?

My tears had gone from the loud kind that are stirred in the heat of fresh grief. Now, they were quiet. Quiet tears come when you have no choice but to move forward both with the known that you wish you could trade and the unknown that you fear. Quiet tears come when you would give anything for your circumstances to change, but you accept moving forward into this new life you would do anything to give back. Quiet tears come from enduring.

Andy told his bosses the medical results of that day: We knew our unborn son had one functioning kidney and a urinoma on the other that was growing. We had just entered the third trimester, but his abdomen was already measuring full term. Unlike most posterior urethral valve cases in which the mothers do not have enough amniotic fluid, I had too much. Doctors kept telling us we were in "uncharted territory." They also told us news we hadn't been able to fully grasp—I would have to move to Houston's Ronald McDonald House when I reached thirty-four weeks of pregnancy. Meaning I would need to leave my four-year-old and two-year-old behind in San Antonio. So we were in a better place than my first doctor in Arizona had predicted, but in terms of how the pregnancy was going, in short: not great.

Later that day, several higher-ups called Andy into a room and asked him to delay his orthodontic residency by a year. They wanted him to be able to focus on our family during this troubling time without the pressure of residency. Andy had the weekend to decide. It was one of the longest weekends of my life. Where I am normally full of opinions, I had none. Of course, I needed Andy. But he had already waited a year and a half to start his program. He made one decision and then felt down. He made the other decision, but still no peace. He looked to me for guidance, and I had none to give. I felt helpless as he held the weight. It was Mother's Day.

Andy and I met when we were both eighteen years old. In our very first conversation, he told me his life plan: to be an orthodontist. How could I tell him to take his bosses up on their offer? He had been waiting for this for more than a decade. And, more than that, the truth was I didn't want to admit our lives had become so heavy again. I didn't want to confess to them, to ourselves, that maybe they were right—we couldn't handle the stress of this pregnancy, delivering in a different city, possible surgery, extended hospital stays, and also the stress of the residency. Our dream of another uneventful pregnancy was already crushed; why did another dream have to come to a halt too?

Our tears that weekend told the truth. That's what tears do. Tears show us the world as it is. Our tears told us it all felt like too much—because it was. Our tears told us we had already endured too much—because we had. Our tears gave breath to our losses—of which we had many.

After consulting several mentors, Andy decided to take the year off from residency and continue working as a general dentist. We realized his residency directors had given us a gift even if it was a hard one to accept. It was Monday, and before going to talk to Andy's bosses, we had to take our son Anderson to the pediatrician. Our pediatrician knew about our unborn son's diagnosis, and through teary eyes, I told him about Andy's decision to delay his residency and asked, "We're doing the right thing, right?"

He responded in a way that I couldn't—that no one could—prepare for: "We had a child die from cancer. You are absolutely doing the right thing."

He did not mean it in a way that conveyed he expected our unborn son not to make it, but instead in a way that said life is precious and unpredictable and we should embrace the time we had been given.

Two days later, we went in for an emergency appointment because I started having contractions while grocery shopping. I winced as the cashier checked me out. We went to my local maternal fetal medicine office, where the team monitored me for a couple hours. The doctor then called me into his office. I sat across his desk when he delivered the news—things were stable but I had to be on partial bedrest. Tears pooled in my eyes; I would have to ask my mom to move in with us earlier than expected, as there was no way to not lift my two-year-old with Down syndrome who was a beginning walker. On the doctor's desk, there was a picture of three young adults. Trying not to think too deeply about my situation just yet, I asked him, "So, you have three kids?" "No, we have four, but we lost our daughter to a rare genetic condition."

That same afternoon we rushed home to interview a respite provider for our children. I liked her right away. She exuded confidence well beyond her years. Then she told us her story: She was a refugee from the Congo who had come to America as a child to escape slaughter.

I was at a point where tears were flowing every day. Salt was a familiar taste in my mouth. Except for my growing belly and a home in a new state, 2017 had not at all turned out the way I expected or wanted. I wanted an uneventful pregnancy. My husband and I had that with our first child. When I was pregnant with Violet, I was blissfully unaware of all the things that could go wrong during a pregnancy. We delighted in my growing belly. We indulged in my many cravings—barbecue, hot sauce, and the occasional late-night ice cream run became a humorous and charming part of our pregnant life.

With our son, Anderson, I had felt none of that. Although I feel very differently about Down syndrome today, I was wrought with grief when we found out about his diagnosis.

It's hard to enjoy someone growing inside of you when you are worrying about what their life will be like twenty years after they are born.

Nearly three years later, I found myself with another growing belly and a fear-filled heart. What if his good kidney looks bad today? What if my excess amniotic fluid makes me go into preterm labor? What if he doesn't make it? What if he will live his life with advanced kidney disease?

Every week I would see him and every week I was worried about him. Every week I worried about us. The dream of another uncomplicated pregnancy had not come true. Add in Andy having to delay his residency plus an impending move away from my children, and the quiet tears flowed and flowed in the ongoing.

These tears did not blur my vision, but instead they were forming a new lens that helped me see with more clarity. This lens helped me to see people in ways I could not without the altered vision. A lens formed through tears shows us there is no remedy for our human fragility. I could see I was connected to these doctors and this respite provider, people who met the end of a road. Through tears, I could see that I was at the end of one of mine. This dream of an uneventful pregnancy would not come true. The dream of a blissful newborn period after a tumultuous one for Anderson would not come to pass. Through tears, I could also see that coming to the end of a road does not mean we have met the end of all roads. New roads had opened up for the doctors and the caregiver. Because I had been at the end of a road before, I knew: An ending is not necessarily the end.

Have you been there too? Has your life veered off path? Maybe you can't even see a path at all. Maybe your tears haven't given you more clarity but instead just more confusion. If you can, begin to loosen your grip on what was or what you thought should be, just a little. Let your tears show you the life you actually have & then let them help you see beyond.

Our lives may not end up on the road we envisioned, but with each curve, there are new opportunities: for new stories to play out, new scenes to take in, new dreams to form. And opportunities to transform into who we are meant to become. My tears were marking the loss of what could have been. The tears were validating the trauma we had endured and were once again enduring. Tears were also helping me see afresh. I could see that these encounters with the doctors and caregiver could not be by chance. Their losses were real. I could see they would give anything to reverse what had been lost & I could see they were not who they once had been because of their losses. They had become a new creation. Perhaps I would too once more. Perhaps you can too.

⸻ & ⸻

Tears have long baffled scientists. Few have devoted research to why we weep, and those who have don't agree on the answer.[1] However, we do know that physiological and psychological research suggests that emotional tears nourish our minds and bodies in ways that surpass common understanding.

A 2015 study aimed to explain the gap in laboratory findings that crying harms our mood & widespread anecdotal reports that people felt better after crying. They showed participants a sad movie and recorded who cried and who did not. As in previous studies, the criers reported increased distress while crying and afterward, while non-criers reported no change. However, when researchers followed up with the crying participants ninety minutes after they left the film, the crying participants reported strong mood improvements. They felt better than they did before crying.[2]

Dr. William Frey reported his findings about crying in his book with Muriel Langseth, *Crying: The Mystery of Tears*. One of his findings was that the protein concentration in emotional tears was 21 percent higher than that found in tears shed in response to an irritant of the eye.[3] Specifically, he found the hormone ACTH present in emotional tears significant because ACTH is a stress indicator.[4] Frey hypothesized that crying is a process by which our bodies excrete stress.[5]

Pastor Ben Perry, author of *Cry, Baby: Why Our Tears Matter*, interviewed Dr. Matthew Pelowski, who studies crying and had this to say: "The literature on crying is moving away from [an understanding that's] purely overwhelming emotion. Maybe that's part of it, but it's cognitive too. It's the process you go through. The tears are a byproduct of getting to a certain point in your dealing with the world."[6]

Tears are pain moving through our beings.

Tears count the cost & tears are our healing in progress.

Tears can help us process what has happened & they can help us to discern a way to move forward in the light of this new reality.

Embracing our tears allows the truth to breathe.

Embracing our tears can lead to transformation, in light of that truth.

--------- & ---------

It was early in the morning. Too dark to see much. Too dark in so many ways. Two nights had passed since He suffered the most heinous death. Two nights had passed since He was buried. It was the third day. She went out of love. She went out of grief. She went to see Him. But the stone covering His grave was gone. She ran, as fast as her legs could carry her weary body. She ran to tell the other disciples the news—Jesus was gone. Someone had taken His body away. Peter and another ran to the tomb to see for themselves. But they could not see. They only saw the clothes that once covered Jesus' body left behind. Then, they left. They went back to the other disciples.

But Mary Magdalene did not. She stayed. She wept. How could there be this hurt on top of hurt? How could someone take Him away? Hadn't He been through enough? Hadn't they all been through enough? As tears still pooled in her eyes, she bent over to look inside the tomb. She saw two angels sitting where Jesus' body once lay. The men missed them. They could only see what was old. Mary's tears gave her a different lens. This lens showed her something new was here, something new was coming.[7]

New Testament Scholar N.T. Wright points to this portion of John 20 as being one of the most comforting passages for the suffering. It is not through clear eyes that Mary Magdalene sees angels but through tears. Wright said, "The misunderstanding is part of the deal. It's people not getting it. And yet Jesus is there. . . . John 20 is all about new creation, but it's about new creation glimpsed through tears."[8]

Through tears, Mary was able to see what the other disciples could not. Her tears did not give her the whole picture. They did not give her all the answers to the questions she undoubtedly had in her heart. However, her tears both held her present grief & pointed her to what lay ahead—a new future.

Later, Mary recognized Jesus in His resurrected body—only after He called her by name. Then He said to her, "Do not hold on to me, for I have not yet ascended to the Father.

Go instead to my brothers and tell them, 'I am ascending to my Father and your Father, to my God and your God.'"[9]

Jesus is telling Mary to let go. The resurrection is not about coming back to our old lives; it's about going forward to new life. Because of Jesus' new life, Mary had a new life too. The road of Mary following Jesus from town to town and listening to His teaching had run out. However, Jesus made a new road for her. She was to take that road back to the other disciples. She was to be the apostle to the apostles. Jesus created an unlikely path for her to be the first witness. In a time when both Jews and Gentiles often questioned the reliability of women's testimonies, Jesus sent Mary to break cultural barriers and expectations.[10] The four Gospels vary in the details of Jesus' resurrection, but this detail is carried out in all four—Mary was the first witness.

Mary's tears marked her pain & through her tears she was given a fresh identity.[11] She would be the first one to tell about the God who suffered with us, for us, & whose story did not end there. He lived. He lives. He who called her by name, who calls us by name, lives. His identity was made complete through the crushing, the tears, and the resurrecting. So too through our tears, Jesus gives us fresh identities—if only we choose to see.

---------- & ----------

We had made the drive many times before for doctor's appointments, only this time, we knew I wouldn't be making the drive back. I was moving to my third town in seven months, and the timeline of my return was still unknown.

We checked into the Ronald McDonald House for the second time in our lives. The first was for a week while Anderson had open-heart surgery. This time, it would be for another son we had yet to meet.

The industrial carpet reminded me of walking the halls of my high school. The small, checkered tile in the bathroom resembled that of a locker room. How could this be home for the next six weeks, two months, maybe longer? How could my children not be here? And yet, how could they be here? Andy and I had dinner reservations at a fancy place for my thirtieth birthday, but I couldn't get the tears to stop flowing, so we canceled.

For two days, I let myself stay in that place. I let myself feel the full depth of the sadness of our situation—me away from the ones who call me "Mommy" so that they could maintain some normalcy, while I got the best care for the brother who would one day call me by the same name. As the scenery became more familiar, the rawness started to wear off. I finally emerged from my room and into the shared living space, where my eyes were opened to the dozens of people also calling this place their temporary home.

At first, I saw families with children with bald heads, feeding tubes, visible disabilities, and invisible illnesses. Then, I let them in. I met the family of a fourteen-year-old with hypoplastic left heart syndrome who had lived at the Ronald McDonald House for months at a time since their son's birth. They shared their homemade tortillas with me. I rode the hospital shuttle with the parents of a child not much older than my oldest who had undergone four heart surgeries in the previous ten months. I ate a meal with a pregnant military mom who had to leave her overseas base to receive fetal surgery for her new daughter with spina bifida.

Most people under that roof were in the middle of one of their life's hardest chapters. For some, the walls were a recurring theme in their stories. This house held sadness, this house held suffering, & it also held joy.

After Andy went back, my mother-in-law flew in to stay with me for a week because I had to have a chaperone for safety reasons due to the nature of my high-risk pregnancy. After dinner one night, we felt a bit unsettled and needed a change of scenery from our room. We crowded around a table with mostly Spanish-speaking families when I saw a heart-wrenching & heartwarming scene: three kids having a tea party with a new tea set one of them had just won at bingo.

The host was a stunning little girl who, had it not been for her purple lips, you wouldn't know was awaiting a heart transplant. She served an imaginary drink to a boy with a facial difference and physical disability that I couldn't iden-tify. Next to him was a girl with no hair who had just won a Disney princess dress that she quickly threw on over her clothes; I had watched her get off the shuttle at the cancer center hours earlier.

They giggled together over pretend sips of tea.

The next day I found myself on the shuttle I normally took to the hospital and instead took it Target. I purchased an Elsa microphone to go with the little girl's dress along with some other toys for the kids at the tea party. Not because I was or am an exceptionally good person but because I had tear-soaked lenses that were helping me see with a higher clarity than I had before. I rode back on the shuttle, excited to deliver the few things I got for the kids.

I was pained & grateful to be a part of it. I was grateful to be with them in the in-between, in the place that held our tears & our hopes. My heart was heavy & my heart was grateful to be connected to the ones who knew this space, a space I had lived in before, a space I was living in again, a space I was ready to leave & a space that I did not want to leave me. Because in this space, everything was more. Life in these in-between spaces plays out in slow motion. Tears make it so your heart sees it all—all the pain & all the joy in all its colors. I was exhausted in the revelation & I was not ready for that lens that showed me them, that showed me myself, that showed me it all to dull.

That night, one of the local businesses sponsoring the dinner brought in a DJ. The same little girl fighting cancer was still in her princess Elsa dress when I handed her a matching microphone and passed out toys to the rest of the table. She danced around her friend who was in a wheelchair; he smiled the entire time.

Their parents sat at a table behind them. The kids and parents were walking through hell and yet they showed me a glimpse of heaven. Perhaps, they experienced a bit of heaven too. The thin veil that separates this world and another is always thin. It is just more apparent in places that hold our tears. These families had run their hands along that veil. Their fingers knew the texture well. I'm sure they had their quiet moments of overwhelming hurt, as well as nights filled with uncertainty and tears, & as they talked and laughed around the dinner table, I saw them holding each other in view of the veil. There was darkness & there was light. They had lenses to see it. Fire allows us to see the world as it actually is—so terrible & so beautiful. Lenses formed by tears allow us to see beyond the veil.

Because Anderson, our son with Down syndrome and a congenital heart defect, had been a part of our lives for more than two years, we were already a part of the disability and medically complex world. The children's illnesses inside the Ronald McDonald House, and the hardships they faced, may have consumed me if it were not for Anderson. But they didn't. Because I already had this new lens. It was still being formed. It was being re-formed with new tears. But I knew the truth that the parents sitting across from me also knew: There is always beauty. Even in shared living spaces far from home, even by bedsides, even in the steps of walking from one hospital wing to another, beauty runs alongside what makes us ache. I too had known the veil. And because of it, because of the tears I had cried while sitting in its presence, I had a lens to see things I might have once overlooked. I belonged. They belonged. We all belong to this God who uses our salty tears to water something new in us.

In case you are wondering if I carried this revelation around every moment of every day, let me assure you I did not. There was a night or two when I did not go down for dinner because it was too much. When my sister arrived to be my next chaperone, there was a night I went to bed at seven because of exhaustion and depression. There was a day my emotions exploded, and I just couldn't ride that shuttle one more time.

& my very human responses did not eliminate what my tears were showing me and how they were re-forming me. It can be this way for you too. Your humanity does not disqualify you from experiencing the holy; your humanity does not disqualify you from becoming.

I wonder what salty tears will water in you.

I wonder what they have shown you or what you will one day see.

I wonder how they will end up changing you.

Maybe one day they will even show you a new road to take.

Of course, I wish our first son never had needed open-heart surgery.

Of course, I wished this son's urinary tract and kidney issues were all part of a bad dream.

Evil does not occur so that we become the people we are intended to be.

Suffering does not exist so that beauty shines more brightly.

& these things can be byproducts of the inevitable pain we experience in this world. I wish my dream of delivering a healthy child had come true.

& because it had not, I was learning to see once again.

Because it had not, because I had been up close to the veil before, I was not who I once was. Because I was there again, I would become new once more. There is no limit on how many times our Creator can make us a new creation.

& for that, I could be grateful.

I could not know the children's future who shared tea. I could not know if the cancer would be cured, if the new heart would last through adulthood, or if the lives of the boys with disabilities would be made better by whatever treatment they were receiving. I don't know how this experience affected their parents. I have a feeling they are people who live life through a tear-soaked lens. A lens that causes us to linger and to see things others often overlook. I have a feeling that because they know pain, they don't turn away from others' pain but see them through it. I have a feeling they stepped out of the Ronald McDonald House different people than when they first crossed its threshold. I have a feeling that through their tears, they became a new creation. If I am wrong, I know this: They are loved by a God who also suffered, and this suffering and resurrected God knows their name.

We are loved by a God who became a new creation so that we could become a new creation too. Our tears can help us to first see differently and then to become different. Our tears can help us to see love and then become love. This trans-formation is not only available in the place beyond the veil but also here. Right here. In hospital beds, at the graveside, and atop our tear-stained pillows. We are not going back; we are moving ahead. We are moving ahead to new life, with a new identity shaped by tears, a new reality shaped by deeper truths we now can see, a new being shaped by love.

FURTHER READING

Psalm 42

❖ REFLECTION ❖

Can you name a time when crying allowed you to see things differently? Mary sat in her grief and through her tears saw angels, while the other disciples left and missed them. What does this reveal to you about how you have handled your grief or are currently handling it? What has the new lens we discussed in this chapter shown you?

& GRATITUDE PRACTICE

I am tired of crying because:

I look back at my most tearful periods with pain in this way & my tears have shown me this:

I have felt lonely in my tears in this way:

I realize how my tears helped me to see others in their tears in this way:

I feel sad God did not rescue me from the pain I have experienced:

I feel hopeful that, like Mary, I will receive a new identity through my tears / I feel grateful for a new identity God gave me through the tears because:

8

Confused & Grateful

THE DAY ARRIVED. We had prepared for this day for months. Only we didn't prep in the way most families do for a new arrival. There was no stocking of diapers or freshly folded newborn laundry. No, our preparation came in the form of multiple doctor appointments each week, MRIs, in-depth ultrasounds, and a move into a Ronald McDonald House almost four hours away. It was the day I would start to bring our son, who we had wept and prayed over, into the world.

The day came earlier than expected. I was only thirty-seven weeks pregnant. However, a week before I had become weirdly itchy. My calves felt as though they had thousands of tiny ants running up and down them trying to build a colony. I developed intrahepatic cholestasis (ICP), which can cause bile acids to spill into blood and tissues, leading to severe itching. ICP also carries a higher chance of birth complications and stillbirth. So the plan changed. The doctors would start the induction process at thirty-seven weeks, just after they performed the fetal intervention surgery.

We also had some other unexpected news. Anderson needed ear tubes, and they couldn't wait. So on the morning of this planned induction in Houston, Andy was with Anderson in San Antonio. He went with Anderson to his surgery, waited for him to come out from under anesthesia, passed him off to my mom, and then drove to Houston to be with me.

We had exited normal a long time ago. When you have been living in Disorder for so long, you forget how something you are experiencing might be a huge deal for someone else. For you, watching your two-year-old have surgery and then driving hours away to go meet your new son who also needs surgery, as Andy did, is somehow not shocking. We knew it was absurd, but we had been living in the land of absurdity for so long that more absurdity was almost expected. Almost laughable, even. Almost.

After I slept in the hospital overnight for monitoring, the surgery began late the next morning. A team of doctors and nurses surrounded me. I lay awake as a large man with hands bigger than my face inserted a needle into my abdomen and through my son's. Quiet tears rolled onto the sides of my temples as a set of noise-canceling headphones playing worship music worked to keep me calm. And I was. I was also uncomfortable, and sad that this was my birth story. The doctor with the giant hands drew out the fluid from my baby's urinoma on his bad kidney as his hands shook from the pressure. At the end of it, there were eleven full syringes.

I felt a wave of relief when it was over. The team smiled; Andy and I smiled too. The first part of the plan they had created months ago was complete. Next, the induction began. I expected it would take a long time, as I was only thirty-seven weeks along, and it did. At one point, a medical student who must not have read our chart came in and introduced herself and told us she would be delivering our baby. She was probably set to deliver *a* baby but definitely not ours, with all his complications. It was hard not to laugh in front of her—thankfully we managed. And then we waited. The waiting opened up space for a fear I had tucked away to come forth. Waiting does that.

We had an amniocentesis done early in the pregnancy because our Arizona doctor was convinced there was something genetically off. The test came back normal. But every doctor we saw after told us to be prepared. In addition to our baby's kidney issues and blocked urethra, he had clubbed feet, and his legs were measuring short.

An amniocentesis can't tell you everything, they warned.

As the technicians poured warm goo over my belly and took out their wands to scan each week, those six words hung over every appointment. They were etched into the darkest parts of my heart, where worry lingered.

We had walked a tough prenatal genetic diagnosis road before. That road transported us into the world of disability. In many ways, we were thankful we had landed there.

However, once you enter this world, you learn things you can't unlearn. You meet people with rare genetic conditions who live different and amazing lives. Yet some conditions are deadly. Months before I got pregnant, I sat in a church and watched our neighbors say goodbye to their two-year-old daughter with a unique set of genes.

On top of dealing with a dangerous diagnosis that was already so complicated, for twenty-three weeks I worried if the specialist's suspicions would be confirmed on this day, our son's birthday.

Per the doctor's request, I labored unmedicated for fourteen hours. Finally, my water broke, and I could tell he was coming fast. The room filled with medical professionals—residents, fellows, nurses, NICU teams, an anesthesiologist who administered the epidural just in time, and even that poor medical student who thought she would be delivering our baby. She was by the door. My husband tells me there were twenty-six people in all. When *the* doctor walked in, it was as if the Red Sea parted. She was a hundred pounds soaking wet and she was revered. She commanded the room with ease.

I was not at ease. This was happening, and it was happening in front of a very large live audience. I was about to see our son for the first time. I wondered if I would know. Would I know if he had a rare set of gene duplications or deletions just by looking at him?

Three pushes and he was out. The tiny doctor yelled to me in her thick Spanish accent as she held him up, "Look, Jillian, look! We're going to assess him right here, Jillian. Look, Jillian—he has hair!"

I'm assuming she could see the blankness stamped across my face. I did not want to look at him. I wondered if this would be the moment my life changed forever—again.

They handed him to me. I kept looking at my husband and asked, "Is he okay?" "Is he okay?" Thinking he would have the answer I wanted. Then, I finally looked at him.

Happiness was absent from that crowded ninth-floor delivery room. Even as the doctor tried to inject some into me through her words, this delivery was all business—the business of surviving. There were no tears of joy & love was breaking through.

Of course we already loved him; we made tough decisions to give him the best care possible. But I didn't *feel* it. I didn't feel the love until he calmly looked into my eyes with a deeply furrowed brow, and I smiled. *He's skeptical, like me.* We laughed.

I didn't feel happy in the delivery room. I didn't get the birth story I wanted. Distress was unavoidable & so was the love. Happiness isn't what carries us through the hard times—only love can do that.

The team took him to the NICU. They let me sleep on the birthing bed for a while before a gentle nurse guided me to the bathroom and helped me clean up the messy parts of bringing forth new life. New life is always messy. A couple hours had passed when Andy rolled me into the NICU. After getting some sleep and eating for the first time in nearly two days, my vision was a bit clearer.

I saw my baby, who still did not have a name, for the first time all over again. He had wires across his body & he was beautiful. I held him to my chest and sobbed. The pain was real, the uncertainty was real, & the love was so very real. That love was no longer just a flicker that I felt in the birthing room; it was fully grown, alive, willing to protect, willing to go to the depths, willing to go to the highest mountain, willing to go anywhere to keep him safe. We named him Preston.

Preston had only been earth-side for a few hours, and it was already time for his first surgery. For eight days, we went round and round with medical procedures and tough conversations with doctors. Our days were spent by Preston's bedside, taking turns making coffee runs, and we even went out to dinner for our eighth wedding anniversary before rushing back. Then, the ninth day in the NICU rolled around. It was the big one. It was the day they would put Preston under general anesthesia to ablate the valves, to remove the blockage in his urethra.

We walked beside his tiny, rolling clear bed to the surgery waiting room. We waited with all the other parents and caregivers. To our surprise, we didn't wait long. The doctor came out, took off his scrub cap, and scratched the top of his head. After inserting a camera in Preston's urethra, they found nothing. The images were clear. There were no valves to ablate. We went home two days later.

—————— & ——————

Just before Preston hit the four-week mark, we descended to a level of hell we had never been to before. A blood draw yielded bad potassium level results, which landed us in the ER for more than six hours of testing, medication, and observation. Preston had casts on his legs to correct his mild case of clubbed feet. On our long day in the ER, we noticed that his toes peeking through the casts looked extra pink. Worried that the casts were too tight, we asked a doctor in the ER if we should have the casts taken off and another set put on. She squeezed his toes, they turned white, then pink again as they are supposed to, and she said they were fine. Two days later, Preston wouldn't stop crying. Hesitant to go back to the ER, Andy finally took him in the middle of the night. A medical assistant took off his casts, and horror was inside. Extreme bruising and blisters were underneath. It would scar and it would scar badly. We were devastated. We were upset with the doctor who missed it, upset with ourselves for not going in sooner, upset Preston was in pain. *How long, Lord?*

When Preston turned six weeks old, and we were still dealing with his cast injuries, we noticed he sounded congested. We went back to the ER for the third time in two weeks; this trip also lasted most of the day, but we were sent home. The next day, we debated about taking Preston in again for the congestion. We talked. We stayed put. And then, he looked gray.

We drove across town, worried, but the real panic set in when we got to the hospital. Nurses from all corners of the ER were swarming to our room. I had never been more scared in my life—not even during Anderson's open-heart surgery. My legs turned into Jell-O. I went out to the hallway, and my legs could not hold me up any longer. My back sliding down the wall, I held my head in my hands and thought, *My son might die, and it will be my fault.*

&

Ecclesiastes is a complicated and at times depressing book in the Old Testament, declaring early on, "Everything is meaningless!"[1] The word *meaningless* appears thirty-nine times in the book and it is the author's chief complaint—that life is futile. The unnamed author, traditionally viewed as Solomon, goes on for twelve chapters interrogating God, who has set up the world in such a way that we don't profit from our efforts. Author Pete Enns says you have to earn your way to read Ecclesiastes: "This is a book for people who have weathered storms, who have seen life and have every reason, so to speak, to be despondent and to be in despair."[2]

Unlike writers of other Hebrew wisdom literature and prophecy, the author of Ecclesiastes finds no meaning or significance in the world's events.[3] One of his larger complaints is that we will all die and will eventually be forgotten. The writer thinks through what it means to hold on to the faith traditions of the past, in light of his present painful reality. The most quoted section of the book holds this tension we must all live with—that life is so full of beauty & so full of pain:

> There is a time for everything,
>> and a season for every activity under the heavens:
>
>> a time to be born and a time to die,
>> a time to plant and a time to uproot,
>> a time to kill and a time to heal,
>> a time to tear down and a time to build,
>> a time to weep and a time to laugh,
>> a time to mourn and a time to dance . . .[4]

The author goes on to say,

> What do workers gain from their toil? I have seen the burden God has laid on the human race. He has made everything beautiful in its time.[5]

Yet, near the end of this chapter, he writes,

> Surely the fate of human beings is like that of the animals; the same fate awaits them both: As one dies, so dies the other. All have the same breath; humans have no advantage over animals. Everything is meaningless.[6]

This text is about coming to terms with the realities of life.[7] The reality of life is this: We will stand in the light and we will know the dark in and out and over again.

> We have to find a way to live in this reality.
> We will experience joy & we will know sorrow.
> We will celebrate beginnings & grieve endings.
> We will live & eventually, no one will remember our
>> names.

Like the author of Ecclesiastes, we will have to come to terms with a God who did not give us the answers for why the world was set in motion in this way. We must come to terms with a God who loved us into being and knew we would experience the whole of this lovely and difficult life.

The book of Ecclesiastes is sobering & it gives us a way to move forward. The book ends in an epilogue:

> Fear God and keep his commandments,
> for this is the duty of all mankind.[8]

This book is largely an interrogation of God & it tells us that we have to eventually lay our questions down. We have to keep going. We have to live knowing there is only so much we can know. We move forward knowing we will experience the depth of what it means to be human. We will know so much pain & we will experience so much joy.

Enns says Ecclesiastes invites us to do the same, "It gives us permission to feel what we're feeling, experience what we're experiencing, and also to relieve us of the pressure of having to figure it out but to move forward anyway, and fear God and keep the commands anyway, or follow Jesus anyway."[9]

Life will continue to be life.

There will be times when life takes us to the highest of mountain peaks & times when it ushers us to the lowest of pits.

Times will be beautiful and joyful & times will be mundane and even tragic.

Times will be peaceful and full of clarity & times will be chaotic and uncertain.

At times, we will see the fruits of our labors & other times fruit will never grow despite our best efforts. At least not the kind we originally planted.

Even the author of this sometimes-depressing book knew this: Despite the pain, and even in the uncertainty, God makes everything beautiful in time.

———— *&* ————

After staying two nights at the children's hospital in San Antonio, Preston recovered from RSV. Days after that hospital stay, it was time to go back for a checkup at Texas Children's Hospital in Houston. This time, we were running tests to see if Preston had a different kind of urinary tract blockage. Preston had to be six weeks old to run the test. We once again handed our tiny baby off to a medical team and waited. But again, no blockage was found.

When we had gone to Texas Children's months prior on Andy's thirtieth birthday while I was still pregnant, we had two days of tests. When all the tests were done, we'd sat with a pediatric urologist, nephrologist, fetal interventionist and maternal-fetal medicine doctor around a table. They had reviewed all the tests and told us they believed Preston had an obstruction in his urinary tract. And yet, no obstruction was found.

When it came time to meet with the urologist that day six weeks after Preston was born, and once again, no blockage was found, I had him walk through our entire pregnancy with us because nothing was making sense. He said everything I described from our pregnancy sounded like Preston had a urinary tract obstruction. When I asked him what happened, he responded bravely and honestly: *I don't know.*

We made the long drive home for the last time. I knew we wouldn't be going back. There would not be a need to go back. We were moving forward. I smiled in disbelief. Andy did too. We sat in the car confused over what God had not done & at what God had done.

God had not intervened in the way we had hoped during the first six weeks of life with Preston. God did not spare him from illness and a medical injury. God did not spare us. & God had seemed to do something beyond anyone's comprehension. The doctors were baffled; we were baffled too. God did not spare our son from all pain & yet our son's life had been spared.

As we passed through the flat Texas land, I realized I had to move forward with a reality I couldn't make sense of. We were standing in miracle territory. A strange, puzzling, and painful miracle. We believed God healed parts of Preston but not all. We did not understand why. We never would. Preston still had clubbed feet, we were still managing his potassium levels, he was still so very fragile, & we were not fighting for his life. He would not live with chronic kidney disease. His lungs were perfect. Medically complex would not be a label he would live with for long.

I believe life has taken you to this in-between place because I think much of our lives are spent there.

Maybe you are in remission & yet treatment side effects still pain you.

Maybe you have experienced the joy of a restored relationship & yet tension lingers.

Maybe you have known successes & still that big dream you are after just doesn't seem within reach.

I believe you know that place we were in, not on the mountaintop, nor in the pit. Instead, in the valley trying to make our way forward.

Before moving to Texas, we lived in valleys for four years, from Nevada to New Mexico and Arizona. I knew this: There are hills in the valleys. We were standing on one of those hills—confused, tired, & grateful. Confused as to how and why God would heal parts of Preston but not all. Tired because of his medical injury and remaining health issues. & grateful that the worst had not and would not come to pass.

The month we found out about Preston's miracle was the same month we had experienced our loss from the year before. In four years, we had one year of peace. It was between heart surgery and a loss. We were not at peace yet. Between my newborn who still had complex medical needs and a toddler with a disability and associated diagnoses, it was common for me to take them to more than ten appointments a week.

However, because I had been in this place before—I knew something even when I could not feel it—I would keep holding on to God, and God would make a way forward. I started most of my days on my old tan couch with an extra fragile newborn. I fed Preston and looked at his injury, his extended belly, & his perfect face. I scanned him and closed my eyes, and was honest with the God who created him, who allowed harsh things to come upon him, & who also protected him. I was honest about my hurt, because I was hurting. Every day felt like a struggle because it was. And then I gave thanks. Because I knew healing had unfolded and would continue to unfold. Both for Preston and for us. God often invites us into a more complete wholeness by way of the splintered path.

You can take this splintered path and struggle with all you have learned and all you will never understand.

You can take this splintered path and let go of the things you are able to let go of that are only weighing you down.

You can take this splintered path forward.

Eventually, it will lead you somewhere new.

Along the way, you can grieve what has been lost, the hardships you still carry, the confusion you feel over it all.

& you can be thankful that there is still a path to walk. This path may not be perfect & yet it is a place where goodness still grows. Because goodness does not run out, not completely.

Like the author of Ecclesiastes, I would never figure out the ways of God, the ways of God in my own life and beyond. I would not understand how God would choose to heal my son and not others in the NICU with the same diagnosis. At the same time, I would not understand why we had been through so much with our sons. I would always live with this tension. I could not answer for my humanity. I could not answer for God. And yet, I knew I could not let go. I knew I would be moving forward anyway with this God I knew and also could not know completely.

We cannot contain an uncontainable God.

We grieve over our real hurts.

We can be disappointed in the God we thought we had.

& we can know this God makes a way forward.

& this forward path will have beauty in it once more.

The mountains would not reach the sky without the earth's core rattling, our bodies kill billions of cells a day that are replaced with new ones, and so too can Disorder kill off parts of us. Disorder can kill good things we hold dear. Disorder can also kill off parts of us that need to die—our certainties, our pride, our strivings to earn our place in the world. Whether our losses are tragic or a necessary goodbye, they make room for God to create something new. Death is a part of our lives & so is new life. New life is messy & new life is beautiful.

When we have walked the splintered path, when we have asked the questions, when we have wrestled with the shadows, when it is time for us to move on, we must first let go. We have to let go of that question that nags us so: *Why?*

We will never find the answer & we can move forward with open hands.

We move forward knowing a more complete picture of this life because we have lived it. We are the ones who have held darkness in one hand & light in the other. We have folded those hands together and somehow whispered prayers— these have been prayers of desperation, prayers of anger, prayers of disbelief, & prayers of gratitude.

As we move forward, we know we will experience death & birth.

We will weep until the salt dries our skin & will laugh until our sides ache.

We will mourn into the darkest part of the night & we will dance until the sun rises.

This is the life we have. It is so often spent right here, right in the in-between, right in the & where things are confusing and messy & where good things never stop growing.

We move forward with the God who loved us into existence before. We can know this God will bring something beautiful out of us again—in time.

FURTHER READING

Psalm 88

❖ REFLECTION ❖

What were you taught about certainty? If you were taught that you had to know what you believed or to never doubt, how has that affected your grief and your faith? If you were taught that questioning God was a good thing, how did that shape your grief and faith? How does embracing the promise of the resurrection in this life make you feel about your past or present grief?

& GRATITUDE PRACTICE

I feel confused that God did not come through for me in this way:

I feel grateful that I learned this in times of confusion:

I feel confused that God is not who I thought, in this way:

I feel grateful that I have learned this about God during my times of Disorder:

I feel confused about the suffering God allows because:

I feel grateful that I could move forward in this way:

Part 3

REORDER

|||||||||||||||||||||||||||||||

There are only two ways to live your life. One is as though nothing is a miracle. The other is as though everything is a miracle.

—Anonymous (though often attributed to Albert Einstein)

9

Scarred & Grateful

TWO YEARS AFTER Preston's miracle, we were deep in the trenches of parenting young children. I managed nap schedules, preschool drop-offs and pickups, and the elementary calendar too. We still had many therapy and doctor appointments. Anderson would undergo two more surgeries in those years, and Preston would undergo two as well. Life was really hard & life was really sweet. We look back at those years and call them our "in-house years." They were filled with repetitive schedules, kitchen dance parties, too much *Sesame Street*, and a whole lot of cuddles. We were grinding at work—Andy in residency and me trying to land a book deal. We didn't venture out much with three kids under five. It was too hard. So we spent nearly all our time under our roof, always together. We had no idea how in-house our lives were about to become. Toward the end of our stay in Texas, the COVID-19 pandemic hit.

Andy's residency came to a halt, and so did the kids' schooling. All the while, I was in the middle of querying literary agents. Much like the rest of the world, we tried to keep the kids busy. Their physical and mental well-being were at the top of our priority list while we tried to maintain our own. As much as we tried to fill the days, we had never had so much downtime. There was a forced pause. There was more time to read. There was more time to reflect. It's probably why my eyes and heart caught it one night while bathing the boys—their scars.

Andy and I had acquired scars raising the boys for the past four-and-a-half years that no one could see. We did not have gashes across our chests, deep indents in our bellies from distension, nor raised tissue on our feet from injuries. Scars for me came in the form of what I believe to be PTSD. I never was formally diagnosed. I had so many appointments for the boys, I didn't have a family medicine doctor for myself in those years, even though I desperately needed one. I believe the stress made me not only mentally unwell at times, but also more physically ill than I have ever been. I remember looking up counselor options but finding the closest to me was forty-five minutes away. With no family support and working for free, I couldn't imagine adding that in. Online counseling was just emerging. Formal diagnosis or not, I remember the day I realized I had been through trauma with the boys. It was the day we officially decided to stop having children.

I was walking to the pharmacy after my husband's vasectomy to pick up his prescription. I was pushing baby Preston in the stroller with one hand and fumbling with my phone in the other when my world suddenly started spinning and I was instantly in a different hospital, in a familiar waiting room, the one where I used to receive one or more ultrasounds a week. My body was in San Antonio; my mind was in Houston.

I had several dizzying flashbacks like that one until they eventually petered out. I thought the symptoms were behind me; the feeling of always waiting for the other shoe to drop lifted. Then I had my first non-pregnancy-related ob-gyn appointment in years, and it hit me again at the sight of three words plastered on the brown door: *ultrasound in progress.*

I watched a woman walk in, my sweaty palms white-knuckled the faux leather chair, while others in the waiting room flipped through magazines. Inside ultrasound rooms, we found a lifelong genetic condition, no heartbeat, and then the last pregnancy, so complicated it forced me to move away from my family for delivery. I watched one woman go in and then come out, then another woman go in and come out. They each left that room with pictures in hand and smiles on their faces. I exhaled the pent-up anxiety, while simultaneously feeling confused, even jealous, at how each woman I saw was happy—no tears, no look of worry on her face.

This only scratches the surface of the scars I wore and wear. My experience alongside my sons' affected not only my mind but my spirit too. The beliefs I once had could not hold in the light of my trauma. Who I once was could not remain. I was unbecoming and becoming while my soul bled and scars formed.

My scars were internal. My boys' scars were on the outside for everyone to see. As I poured the water over their heads and rubbed tear-free soap into their skin, I realized that one day they would ask me about their scars. What would I say? Would I tell them that it was part of God's plan? Or would I tell them I would take it all back if I could? What did their scars mean? What did my scars mean moving forward?

———— & ————

We all have scars, and we continue to acquire them throughout our lives. A scar, usually composed of fibrous tissue, is the body's response to "the natural healing process of wounds or trauma."[1]

The scarring process has four stages.

The first is *hemostasis,* in which blood rushes to the wound and begins clotting to stop the bleeding.

The second stage is *inflammation.* When hemostasis is effected, cells come in to repair the wound.

In stage three, *proliferation,* as new tissues are built, the wound contracts, and cells cover the wound.

The final stage is *remodeling.* After around twenty-one days, the deeper structures begin to form to give the wound area strength; the process can continue for about two years.[2] *Two years.*

Our bodies are miraculous. God designed them in such a way as to sometimes cure themselves. However, the deeper healing, the strength that comes after we are wounded, often takes time. Healing is not only done at the surface level where we were wounded, but also deep below where we cannot see. Healing begins in the darkness and ushers us toward the light. The healing work of God is often slow & the healing work of God is always in process.

———— & ————

Although we see Jesus cure people in an instant many times in the Gospels, there are two examples of miracles that unfold more slowly. One of those times is seen in Mark 8, where Jesus heals a blind man in Bethsaida.

He had just fed more than four thousand people, but the work was not done. He climbed into a boat with His disciples and moved on.

A familiar request pierced the air. A group of Pharisees asked for a sign. They had proof, but it wasn't enough. It never would be.

Again, they pushed the boat off the shore. He would teach His followers while on their way to teach others. "Watch out for the yeast of the Pharisees and that of Herod." The disciples didn't get it. They started searching the boat for bread.

Jesus said to them, "Do you have eyes but fail to see, and ears but fail to hear?" He wasn't talking about food. He wasn't talking about their physical abilities. He was talking about their spiritual sight—how they saw the world, how they saw Him.

They arrived on the shore of Bethsaida and were greeted by a group of people with a blind man among them. Jesus took the man away from the crowd. Jesus spit on his eyes and put His hands on the man. "Do you see anything?" He asked. The man said he saw people, but they looked like walking trees. Jesus put his hands on him one more time. His eyes were opened. He saw people. He also saw his healer staring back at him. He saw clearly.[3]

The blind man once only saw darkness, and then the light broke through, but this light only showed partial truth. As he spent more time with Jesus, more time in the light, his sight was further restored. First the darkness, then the light, and after we spend time in the light—a more complete healing unfolds.

Theologian John Swinton writes that the closest word to *health* in the Bible is *shalom.* "Shalom is not the absence of illness, disease or disability. It has to do with the *presence* of God. . . . *Healing always has first and foremost to do with connecting and reconnecting people to God.*"[4]

I think that by Jesus healing the man in this way, He is trying to show us something about our own healing. True healing is more than a change in condition. It is about experiencing and embodying shalom. It takes spending time in the light to know God, and to know God is to know peace, love, justice—and to know ourselves.

The disciples also needed a second touch for their eyes to be opened. They needed to spend more time in the light to be more deeply connected with their Creator. The disciples were in God's presence and they walked with Him and talked with Him, but they were unable to fully connect because they were trying to make sense of Jesus in light of their old tradition. But Jesus came here not to fit into the old but to break out and do something brand new. The disciples were beginning to see, but their vision was still blurry.

Clinton E. Arnold writes, "The disciples saw dimly in a glass coated with the dust of traditional ways of viewing things and warped by the curvature of their dreams and ambitions. The glass we look through is no different. We are no less in need of healing before we can see what God is doing, and it may not take on the first try."[5]

Healing goes deeper than our immediate want. Healing changes us from the inside. Healing comes when we recognize we are loved and we are meant to be transformed by this love. Healing happens when transformation goes beyond ourselves and starts pushing us toward the way of love. Healing happens when we begin to see ourselves, to see God, not through our old lens, but through a new one shaped by scars. Healing is God revealed to us and in us, and that requires our time, our honesty, and our gratitude.

Going back to Walter Brueggemann's format of the Psalms in *Spirituality of the Psalms*, we have now arrived at the point of New Orientation, or as we are calling it, Reorder. Brueggemann writes this about the Psalms of New Orientation: "All these prayers and songs speak of the intervening action of God to give life in a world where death seems to have the best and strongest way. The songs are not about the 'natural' outcome of trouble, but about the decisive *transformation* made possible by this God who causes new life where none seems possible."[6] We enter Reorder when we have a heart ready to see how God breathes new life into what seems dead.

New life requires our gratitude. Without gratitude, our hearts will only count our losses. True gratitude doesn't gloss over our hard things; instead it looks for the ways new life is unfolding right alongside them. Without gratitude, we miss this new life and end up living in Disorder. Disorder is necessary & Disorder is not meant to be a permanent destination.

After we leave our time of Disorder, we don't step back into our old lives, but into new life. We cannot go back to old belief systems that do not hold in the light. We cannot go back to our old ways of living, as if life is all up to us. We cannot go back. Instead, we stand in this new light and walk toward a new life marked by shalom. We walk there with hearts that have been broken & mended, with bodies that have been cut & fused back together & we walk there scarred.

We do not have to glamorize trauma. What doesn't kill us can harm us quite deeply. We do not have to tie our traumas up in neat bows lined with silver & we can walk in this new life knowing that healing has never stopped. As we were hurting, our Creator was slowly working in the dark, pulling us back together in a way that would leave us marked & also changed. The scars we wear are fresh as we emerge from death to life. Fresh scar tissue has less elasticity and is not as strong as normal tissue & we know that in our weakness, we are made strong.[7] In our softness, we are made new.

&

I looked at my beautiful & scarred boys. They will wear their scars on their bodies for the rest of their lives. I knew I would wear mine on my heart for the rest of mine. I poured the water over their sweet heads one more time as a tear quietly rolled down my cheek at the realization: We would all be marked by the trauma we endured together.

I couldn't—nor can I—wrap up chest tubes and nephrostomy bags in pretty packaging. The truth is, if I could have taken away the pain my boys experienced, I would have. I still would. I would take away the days in the hospital and trade them for mornings on our old couch. I would take away the burning pain from incisions and trade them for restful nights. I would take away the distrust they had of medical professionals, the distrust they maybe even had of me, and wrap them in a security blanket. I am their mother and I would trade away their trauma if I could. But I cannot.

In this life, we will know hurt, & living in the light Jesus brings, we can look back at our pain and know He was pursuing our healing the whole time. Because He has been pursuing us from the beginning of time. Because we cannot have lived our days in hospitals, custody courtrooms, or at the funeral home and walk away the same. The thing is, we either become hardened versions of ourselves, only seeing what our circumstances took from us, or, through gratitude, we can look to see what that experience also gave us. With honest gratitude, we can count the cost & look below the surface and know that God was slowly healing us, bringing us closer to Godself. In this life, we will have scars. We have a God who wears them too. Jesus' scars define Him. Jesus without scars would be incomplete. Jesus with scars is Jesus in His entirety. So too it can be this way for you.

The blind man would always be marked by his experience of being disabled in a time when society viewed disability as a moral failing. He undoubtedly experienced oppression. He undoubtedly was made to feel less than by those who did not love him. The pain of our past is not erased by healing. It marks us. Yet, I wonder what the man let his scars show? Would he go back to society and try to fit into those norms that once put him on the outside? Or would he walk forward with a God who restored his physical sight so he might see afresh spiritually? With his new sight, would he take on the old lens of exclusion and rules or would he wear this new Jesus-soaked lens? A lens that shows us this: God came here not to exclude, punish, or dominate, but to love us into healing.

We are meant to live into and out of this love. When we love, when we see that love is the force that hems us in, when we know love is the reason we are all here, then we are healed. This God was not only available to those who wore robes and performed the trademarks of the holy. This God comes close. This God gets in the dirt with us. When the blind man came into his sight, he came face-to-face with a God who would eventually wear His own scars.

We shouldn't try to mask our scars, but instead should ask ourselves, What do we want them to show? Will they only mark our pain? Or will we allow them to mark our healing too? Our scars can be a pathway. With their jagged edges, they remind us of where we have been, places we may not have chosen, and yet miraculously, we live.

Our scars mark an ending & our scars can mark a new beginning.

One day, I will tell my boys what they have been through and what their scars mean. I will tell them of the trials they have already withstood. I will tell them that if I could have spared them the pain, I would have. & I will tell them this: These scars they wear will not be the only ones. To live is to love & to live is to lose. To live is to know beauty & to live is to feel pain. To live is to experience small deaths & thankfully, to live is to experience new life. As they move on in life, I hope that they will look back & that they will look up. They have risen once, and they can rise once more. They will rise scarred. We rise scarred. Hopefully, we rise changed too. It is in this way we can look at our scars and feel gratitude.

Scars mark our losses & scars show us all we still have.

Scars mark our pain & scars point to our healing.

Scars mark our humanity & scars reveal the Divine working deep within.

Scars mark our fragility & scars guide us toward a gentler kind of strength.

The strength that comes from scars is vulnerable.

I am more vulnerable & I am stronger than I once was because of my scars. I have experienced shalom through these scars—because they have drawn me toward a more interconnected life. My scars remind me of all I have lost & all God has done. Although I sometimes feel sad, even now, when looking back, I also feel grateful. My scars have changed me in ways that are mostly good. My scars have allowed me to see others in pain more clearly than I once did. I am connected to those in need because I have been in need. It is my scars & my gratitude that allow me to see and call me to act. I volunteer in spaces I never would have otherwise. I get involved in causes I never knew about before. I love differently and more deeply than I once loved.

This is possible for you too. You can look at your scars and see your pain & also your healing. It requires you to see what God has done and what God is doing. It might not take on the first try. Like the blind man, like the disciples, you may need a second touch. And possibly a third, a fourth, and beyond. I did.

Once you get to this place, a place where your vision becomes clearer, a place where you can see your scar on the surface and also know what has happened below—you can experience shalom. Shalom is not the absence of pain. Shalom is not the absence of scars. Shalom is knowing the presence of God, and God is Love.

I believe your scars can help you to experience Love in ways you did not know before you were scarred.

When life takes hold, look at your scars. When you can't see forward, look at your scars. When you feel out of hope, look at your scars. Look at your scars and see how far you have come. See how far God has already taken you. Look at your scars not to live in your past but to remember this is not where your story ended. Look and see how your ideas have begun to change. Look and see how your perspective has shifted. Look and see how you have an even more tender heart that wants to help others in pain. Look and see how these wounds have hurt you & also how God has healed you through them.

Your scars can give you much if you look at them through the lens of gratitude.

Because healing demands gratitude.

Healing requires you to stand in the light again and again.

Healing requires you to notice how new life is unfolding when it once seemed impossible.

There God was, working in ways you could not see.

& yet now you do.

God somehow brought new life out of what seemed dead and continues to do so in your life and beyond.

The more time you spend in this light, the more you will see new life burst forth.

This light will connect you to the One who created you and to the ones you were made to love.

The more you stand in this light, the more you will be healed.

We do our best to stand in this light & stand here scarred.

FURTHER READING

Psalm 30

✤ REFLECTION ✤

How did you feel about your internal or physical scars be-fore reading this chapter, and how do you feel about them now? What are your thoughts on our participation needed for deeper healing that brings us closer to God? Scars mark our pain & they can mark our transformation. In what ways do you feel your scars leading you to transform?

& GRATITUDE PRACTICE

I feel pain when I examine my scars in this way:

I feel grateful for the healing my scars show in this way:

I feel a sense of loss over what I now cannot unsee in this way:

I am grateful for the new lens I have received in this way:

I would give back things that scarred me because:

I am grateful for the new life I see coming out of the darkness in this way:

10

Trust Looks Different Now & I'm Grateful

WE WERE A MONTH into the pandemic, and I was curling my hair one morning. I sectioned it off piece by piece, hoping the normalcy in the mirror would help me to claim a sense of it during yet another lock-down day. That's when I felt it. While pressing a 400-degree iron next to my temple, I felt a strong knowing for the second time in my life. The first happened when I met Andy on the steps of his University of Georgia fraternity house. It was as if the scenes around me faded, the sky tilted in, tunneling us both. Our conversation unfolded sweetly and slowly, like molasses dripping off a spoon; it felt as if God was tapping me on the shoulder, telling me, *This is important*. This time, as I wrapped my dirty blond strands around the hot barrel, I felt these words: *Let me give you this gift.*

I needed that assurance, as rumors had started swirling in our corner of the Air Force due to the pandemic halting certain types of medical care, including orthodontics. Andy was unable to see patients at the time, and we'd heard there might be an early path out of the military and into private practice. We had just met with a potential business partner in Florida, close to where I grew up. He said he would wait for us to start the partnership, but would he? Andy's Air Force separation date was three years away, and that's a long time to wait. So we wondered, *If a path to leave the military early became available, should we take it?* Because taking it would mean missing out on our dream base assignment we had just received—Colorado Springs, Colorado. We obsessed over the possibilities because what else did we have to do with our time? The inaudible, knowing nudge from God was a stop sign for the worry and wonder. A sign to embrace the gift of our current plan.

After five military moves, we were supposed to unwrap the gift of the Rocky Mountains we had dreamt of for so long. We interviewed school principals for Anderson via Zoom. We bought our first house from our Texas living room. We set up the boys' medical care by making too many phone calls. We were ready to unwrap this gift.

My mom and niece flew out to help with the move while Andy wrapped up things in Texas. We made the thirteen-hour drive through Texas's flat and sometimes very dry land, and then we hit a stop in our past—New Mexico. We drove past rusty orange plateaus and tan plains. My stomach flip-flopped as we drove away from the sight of our before-and-after moment and the sight of the ongoing—wanting to believe we were heading somewhere different this time. Hope felt scary.

Our minivan crossed into Colorado. The view made the Southwestern mountains I once knew seem small, and we were barely over the state line. Could this be happening? Were we moving into a new phase, a new life? Was this the promised land? A land where our time would not be marked by Disorder like the last five years, but by something else? Something good? Could God not only be good, but good to *me*? I wanted to trust, but we had trusted before, only to be met with unwelcome detours that left us in unrecognizable territories. I trusted, and the heartache came for me again and again. What did it mean to trust in a God who had said *no*, who had given a miracle, who had remade me, yes, but had remade me allowing Disorder to break me again and again?

———— *&* ————

The disciples did what He asked. They borrowed a donkey and a colt to fulfill what had been said long ago. Then, He made His entrance into the city. The people laid their cloaks on the road for His triumphant arrival into Jerusalem. They cut branches off trees and laid them down because royalty doesn't touch the ground. The crowd shouted, "Hosanna!" Meaning, "Save us!" For that's what they wanted. They thought this was the one who would rescue them from Rome's heavy heel. They were tired of being crushed and drained by their oppressors. They were tired & they were hopeful. Hopeful that this man, this mortal who was in touch with the miraculous, would be their answer. This man would be their king.[1] This king would put an end to the pain. This king would raise them up from the depths. And because this king had God on His side, God would be on their side again. This king would not only listen to their cries for rescue, He would deliver the Promised Land to them once more.

But this King would not be taking a seat on the throne. He would not be raising a military to fight. Instead, He was marching toward

His death. In doing so, He was inviting them into a new kind of king-
dom, a new kind of life. The people would not be saved from Rome.
This was not the rescue mission they thought it was. This King would
not overturn violence with violence. This was a King who would rule
by love and He would do so by dying.

The Israelites wanted a king like their hero kings from long ago—a military leader who would fight and overthrow their oppressors. They wanted someone new to restore them to the old—to back when things were good. They wanted a savior to protect them from the worst the world has to offer. So too it is with us.

Even Jesus' closest followers wanted a militant messiah. Daniel Kirk, a New Testament professor at Fuller Seminary, writes, "The twelve were committed to Jesus, and happy with him—but only as one who came with power. They lacked faith to participate in his way of death. They did not have eyes to see that the ministry of Jesus turned the economy of the world on its head."[2] The disciples wanted a powerful king, not a king who would give up power and choose death. What kind of king would do that? They did not understand the subversive ways of Jesus.

In the book of Mark, Jesus warns the disciples about His impending death three times. The first time, Peter rebukes Jesus for suggesting such a thing.[3] The second time, the disciples did not understand and were too afraid to ask Him about it.[4] The third time, James and John ask Jesus for power—they want to sit next to the ruler.[5] They missed it. They trusted they had a king ready to overturn Rome. They trusted He would rule the land and they wanted to rule alongside Him.

Later in Mark, there is one person who gets it. There is one person who understands that messiahship and death are tied together.[6] Days before Jesus' death, while Jesus was eating at a home in Bethany, an unnamed woman broke a jar of expensive perfume and poured it over Jesus' head. The disciples rebuked her for being wasteful. Jesus admonished them, saying, "She poured perfume on my body beforehand to prepare for my burial. Truly I tell you, wherever the gospel is preached throughout the world, what she has done will also be told, in memory of her."[7]

This outsider of a woman trusted the compassionate way. Jesus was not a king with a sword to inflict pain, but a King who would choose to bear it. In this kingdom, the grieved, broken, and outcast are called blessed.[8] In this kingdom, the hurting are closest to the heart of God, not the farthest away. In this kingdom, suffering is not the desire of the King & it is a pathway to know Him more deeply.

The people wanted a king arriving on a warhorse.
Instead, they got a King who arrived on a donkey—a symbol of peace.
The people wanted a king to overthrow the government.
Instead, they got a King who allowed the government to take His life.
The people wanted this king to return them to the way it used to be.
Instead, this King came to do something brand new.
Jesus didn't come here to rescue us from our humanity.
Instead, He joins us in it.

When we look for militarized King Jesus to save us, we won't find Him. When we look for the Jesus who laid down His power to show us the greater love at work, we do. Once we have been through Disorder, we might not find the God of rescue we once believed in. We find the God of Instead.

&

On the Christian calendar, there is one day set aside to acknowledge Jesus as King. It is the final day of the church calendar before Advent—the four-week reflective celebration of Jesus coming to earth and anticipatory hope of Jesus coming to earth again. Before we walk into new life, we must come to terms with the King we actually have.

We want a king to rescue us because our lives can get so very chaotic. We want someone to fix it. We want someone to defeat the threat that is pressing us. We want someone to raise us to God-like status, so we can escape our humanity and avoid pain. We forget that we have a God who entered into pain. As they nailed His hands, spit on His skin, and hung a sign above His head that said "King of the Jews" to humiliate Him, He did not show His mighty ability and instead displayed the ultimate humility. This King chose to die instead of kill.

This King brought all things into being and sustains all things through love *&* yet bad things happen here. This God does not always rescue us from turmoil; He did not rescue Himself. Yet, through love, He brings new life out of the Disorder. Through love, the world keeps spinning.

Reverend Taylor Fuerst says, "In Christ the King we find not the king who shields us from threat, but rather the one who stands among the threatened. What we find is not the God who plucks us out of the storm but the one who enters the storm with us."[9] Jesus chose the vulnerable way because there is no love without vulnerability. Jesus chose the way of love.

Love does not always rescue.
Love does not always make cancer go away.

Love does not put an end to every evil.

Love does not force.

Instead, Love draws us closer when the sky turns black.

Instead, Love surprises us with bursts of beauty.

Instead, Love meets us where we are and promises to not leave us the same.

This is why I have come to know our Creator as the God of Instead.

If I could sit across from you now, I would tell you that I once thought to trust God meant that I would be safe. I was wrong. In the light of what God has shown me, I now walk with an open heart, knowing it will one day break again & I am trusting God's grace not only to put my heart back together but to expand it in the remaking. We keep walking vulnerably, knowing goodness is here, that pain will one day come again & so too will new life. This is the resurrected way.

When I was told my four-month-old needed open-heart surgery, I wanted the God of miracles. Instead, I found a God who most often works through the hands of ordinary people called to the extraordinary.

When I found myself bleeding while eight weeks pregnant, I wanted the God of rescue. Instead, I found the God who offers comfort when the world goes dark.

When I found myself pregnant again with a baby who would require fetal intervention surgery, I wanted the God of fair. Instead, I found Grace somehow helping me move forward after experiencing heartache once again.

Time and time again, I have wanted the God of rescue & time and time again, I have found the God of Instead. Jesus may not work the way we want. Instead, He surprises us by stepping in with people He puts on our paths. Instead, He surprises us by wrangling goodness out of the unimaginable. Instead of changing our circumstances, He often changes us. He points to the scars on His own hands and then to the scars we wear. He reminds us that yes, life hurts & goodness breaks through. He breaks through.

We drove deeper into Colorado toward our new hometown. It was hard to keep my eyes on the road and not stare at the beauty enveloping me. I wanted to trust. I wanted to know what trust looks like once you know you have never really been safe. But there, in my gray minivan, with my kids wired and ready to burst through the doors of their new home, I was held in the beauty of a new beginning, whatever it might bring.

I crossed the threshold of our new house for the first time. It was our sixth home together and the very first one we owned. It was just as beautiful as the pictures promised. Maybe even more so. The kids ran around the empty space soon to be filled. I teared up, looking at the hardwoods and the shiplap, knowing this place we just stepped into was different. Those tears held my gratitude. Having stepped over the threshold, I knew I was entering a new phase of my life, our lives—I trusted that hard & wonderful things would happen here. And they did. Mostly wonderful.

I no longer trust that God will rescue me from my humanity. Instead, I trust in a God who will love me through it. Instead, I trust in a God who will take my hand and point me toward new life. There is no resurrection without death. I wish there were another way. But this is not the life we have. This is not the life God designed. Instead, this God promises that death is not the end—whether that death is after the final breath we take or when we experience the end of something or someone we loved. We can trust that every ending has a new beginning. From seeds that are planted to babies growing in the womb, we can trust that new life is born out of darkness. We can trust that no matter what happens in our lives, we are held, we are loved, and we will be made new by the God of Instead.

-------- *&* --------

Morning after morning, I hit brew on the coffeemaker before the kids woke up. It was summer, so the mornings were bright even when the kids still had their eyes closed. I would take my hot, semisweet concoction and head for the front door. What would the view look like today? Would it glow in pink and purple? Would it just be bright, bouncing golden sun? No, instead, for weeks the sky was covered in a thick haze. I sat at my yellow and blue mosaic table, the same table I had been sitting at most mornings since our first apartment five moves prior. We wanted to live in Colorado for the mountain views and instead were greeted by smoke drifting over from other burning parts of the West. The world was burning. It always is. Until one morning, the smoke in our corner of the world was gone. There she was again: Pike's Peak. Purple, orange, pink, green, gray and just a hint of white snow at her very top even in June. She was beautiful. She had never stopped being beautiful. I just couldn't see her through the haze. The mountain never moved.

When Disorder comes, it can create a haze so thick that it hides the source of life itself. It's where we experience endings, death—death of parts of us, death of what could have been, death of what we think should have been. And yet, transformation often begins to unfold when we are at our lowest point, far from the mountain.

As time moves, the pain we endure can chisel away our most hardened parts and soften what remains. The smoke that clouded our vision begins to clear.

The heavy haze was real & the mountain never left. We just couldn't see when we were being pressed, when we were in the beginning, painful phases of becoming new.

When the haze lifts, the mountain does not return to us. We return to the mountain, changed. And when that day comes, we are thankful not only to see the mountain again but also to know it was there all along. Colorado was a gift. It was the promised land. Not because it was seamless. It was because I was finally beginning to see what it is that God promises: resurrection.

There were times in Disorder where I could see it—I could see signs of new life blooming at my feet and up ahead. There were also times I could not. Although I believe our lives largely flow from Order to Disorder and Reorder, life is not always linear. Healing is not linear. Some days we can see, and sometimes we can experience the resurrection life in times of distress. And then there are times when the haze is too thick. But even when we cannot see, we can know. We can know that even when everything is unclear, God is planting new life in the darkness. Through God's own death & resurrection He promises us we will also know death & resurrection. He will make something new out of this, something new out of us. The process has already begun, and is always unfolding.

The resurrected life is not a perfect one. The resurrected life is still life. It comes with fire now and again, and the smoke is not an illusion. The resurrected life is not the absence of smoke; it's the recognition that the mountain does not move even when we cannot see its glorious peaks. When the smoke clears we see a bit differently than we used to. We see the world not through rose-tinted lenses, but with magnifying ones. We see the world as it is, broken & beautiful. We lean into both. We live our lives trusting that one day all things will be beautiful. We play a part in making beauty a reality while we wait—in our own lives and in the lives of others.

The mountains are birthed out of extreme conditions, often through the death of one landform and the resurrection of a new one. We have a God who revealed His fullest self through death and resurrection. We too can become like the mountains—scarred, beautiful, and new.

I'm thankful we lived in Colorado as if we were running out of time. Because, unbeknownst to us, we were. There was a quicker path out of the military. We took it. But I will not forget the gift that those fourteen months were. We took a weekend trip to Telluride and wondered at all her orange, green, and gray landscapes. We taught our daughter how to ski. We chose hiking over kids' sports. We sledded down the tiny hill in our backyard with a toddler who looked like a bouncing baby seal. We breathed. We were held in beauty & we were held in our disappointments. We were held in it all.

Colorado showed me gorgeous mountain views.

Colorado had my kids falling in love with nature as they climbed rocks.

Colorado hemmed me in with her mild summers and vibrant falls.

&

Colorado was a time of loneliness off a fresh move in the middle of a pandemic.

Colorado was sometimes dark and very cold in the dead of winter.

Colorado was a time of rejection, as my first book got
turned down.

&

Colorado was all together beautiful.

It was beautiful not only because of its gorgeous landscape
that would sing to my soul if not every day, then most of them.
Colorado is where I began to love the God of Instead. When I
was rejected by a dozen publishers, I felt sad and embarrassed
& because I had been in the depths of the Disorder before, I
also knew this: It was not over. The night I got the news of
the final rejection, I lay in bed, writing a social media post as
tears quietly fell. Those two hundred words were shared by
hundreds of people who needed the message: Life moves on,
and it's by God's grace we move on—changed. Though crying,
I knew this was the way forward. These words would guide
me. God was guiding me through them. I would not publish
the book I had spent more than a year writing; instead, these
words would reshape that message. These words were the
ones I had not yet known. They were the path further onto the
way of instead. They would not only be a part of the introduction of my revised book but would transform the book entirely.

I went to bed that night, still with tears in my eyes &
knowing that out of this small death, new life was stirring
once more. Death happened that day & so did resurrection. I
went to bed still sad & with a grateful heart. Not because God
rescued me. Instead, God brought something new out of me,
and I trusted this newness was leading me somewhere good.

This is how it can be for you too.

You will know endings & beginnings. You will grieve and
maybe even question the endings & you can co-create new
beginnings with the One who created you.

I wonder how honest gratitude will take you into new life—a life you may not have imagined, a new life marked by instead.

Maybe the systemic pain you experienced will call you to the work of justice.

Perhaps the loss of a loved one will have you showing up for others who know losses as deep as yours.

I wonder if navigating the complex world of medical care will lead you to a new career path or perhaps to just being there for someone coming up behind you who will need another to guide them.

I pray you have eyes to see it all—the totality of your hurt & what God has instead planted in the places that once felt empty.

We cannot trust that God will rescue us from our humanity & instead, we trust that God will not leave us in our fragility.

We cannot trust that Disorder won't come for us again & instead, we trust that when our hearts break, God will help us build something new with the fractured pieces.

We cannot trust that the will of God will bend toward our will & instead, we trust in a God who promises new life.

I trust in God. I trust in the God who does not always save us from death & instead promises resurrection, in the next life, and this one.

I trust in new life made possible by Love.

I trust the God of Instead.

Thanks be to God.

Further Reading

Psalm 40

❖ Reflection ❖

What did trusting God look like before your time in Disorder, and what does it look like now? How does the term *God of Instead* resonate with you? What would it take for you to come to terms with the King we actually have?

& GRATITUDE PRACTICE

I feel disappointed that God did not come to rescue when:

I am grateful for a God who loved me like this during that time:

I have a hard time trusting goodness will follow me because:

I am grateful I can look back and see new life coming out of dark times in this way:

I miss being able to trust that life worked like this:

I am grateful my views have changed in this way:

11

Life Is Not What I Imagined
& I'm Grateful

FALL 2022
FLORIDA'S SPACE COAST

BEFORE THE GIFT that was our time in Colorado, I remember when we were on my hometown beach in Florida for a spring vacation in 2018. It was baby Preston's first time. I couldn't get enough of his fat dimpled hands grasping the sand and then letting the small beige pebbles fall through. I couldn't get enough of his giggles as he threw that sand and then laughed with glee. I couldn't get enough of life that day. I was in a place where I felt robbed of his babyhood. Just like his brother's babyhood before him, his was not spent at baby playdates or toddler time at the library or even running errands. We spent our days at the doctor's office and therapy appointments.

But not this day. This day, I was his mom. This day, he was my sweet baby discovering the beach for the first time. I sat on the shoreline by myself as the waves lapped my feet. They rolled in and out whispering, *Home, home.* The message confused me. I was the teenager who wanted to leave my hometown as quickly as possible. I was an insufferable senior—I just wanted to get to the good part. The next part. I wanted new.

Now, the shore was calling me back.

A few months later, back in Texas, Andy received a text message from the orthodontist he had shadowed several times since dental school—two towns over from where I grew up—they started discussing a partnership. We wondered, *Would Florida be our home?* Then, in March 2020, days before the pandemic shut the world down, we met with him and his wife to discuss a possible future together. After that meeting, we had gotten into our car, and Andy looked at me and said, "This is it." The wondering of where we would end up could stop. He knew it was the right move. We just hoped the orthodontist would wait for our military commitment to be up.

Because of the COVID-19 pandemic, the military had too many members, so it expanded a program that allowed service members to substitute active duty years for time in the reserves, meaning Andy could separate from active duty and pay back his remaining commitment through the reserves instead, which would free us up to move to Florida. After many obstacles in that process, we were in disbelief when we actually got it. We sat in the dark in our Colorado home the night we got the news. We sat mostly in quiet, the hum of the gas-lit fire filling the air.

I felt sad & relieved. Sad because the gift of Colorado was so short-lived. Sad because I knew Anderson was at the right school and I didn't know what school awaited us. Sad because it was the end of an era. During our military years, we lived in five states over eight years. We built our family. We experienced the immense joy that comes with that. We also experienced so much heartache with unexpected diagnoses, hospital stays, and loss. The military years stretched us and grew us and taught us how to love each other well because oftentimes we were all we had. Our military years also taught us to be adventurers and to make the most of the little time we were allotted in each location. We had opportunities we never would have had otherwise. The military years broke our hearts and put them back together again.

Now, they were over. There was relief in that too. Relief because my husband had just watched my dreams come true with a book contract signed, and now it was his turn. Relief because military life is hard. Relief because for the first time in our lives we would have built-in support, as my parents would live less than an hour away. My complex emotions danced among the flickering flames. The news brought loss & it brought gain. I remembered those whispering waves from years before. *Home,* they had called, and home we would go.

It might have been home, but I have never escaped the post-move blues. I knew we were where we were supposed to be, and yet after living nearly half of my life away from the place where I was raised, I felt a bit suffocated being back in the same county. It didn't help that the house we bought sight unseen was a little worse than what the pictures portrayed. My mom saw the house in person and warned me. But we had a tight timeline, and I could only get one school recommendation from the disability community that was practicing school inclusion. This *had* to be the house. But nothing quite prepared me for the animal smell left over from the previous owners, feces still left on the carpet. There were mismatched floors from room to room, and the paint was two decades old. We stepped into a project.

We would have to rebuild not only the house but our lives. Only this time, this home, this place, was not temporary. This was the site of our forever. We had never been in a place long enough to grow deep roots. Before, the wind would blow and we were plucked from the ground that temporarily became home and replanted somewhere new—only to do it all over again. This was different.

About two weeks after moving in, we met another family that had a child with Down syndrome on the beach. I'd had no idea how close we were to the beach—that's how quickly we'd had to move. It was that thirteen-minute drive down a road that made it feel like we were deep in the tropics, then being greeted by the whispering waves once more, that lifted the blues. *Home,* the waves said. Home, they pulled me in. Home is where we landed.

Most of life felt shiny on Florida's sunny shore. Andy and I walked the beach nearly every Friday morning, just in awe of how we got here. We walked on holy ground. For years, we dreamt up where we would eventually land. And here we were. No longer in transition but instead in a place of permanence. Life was in many ways what we imagined it to be—Andy a private-practice orthodontist, and me a published author. I took so many pictures, too many pictures, of that time. I captured the seashells and took videos of the scurrying crabs. I even got a few shots of dolphins, including one jumping out of the water like Flipper. It felt as if God was smiling at us. We were fresh in the newness of God just like we were after we said our vows and in the glow of the hospital lights after the birth of our first child. We were new again, yet this time it was different. We were new in a way that we could not look at the world with unknowing eyes of twenty-somethings. We knew too much. We had been through too much. We also knew how little we knew. The need for certainty ceased, and we were content to stand in the mystery of God's goodness. We were thankful for how God had written our story home.

& we carried the things from the unexpected years with us.

When we got to Florida, one of the first things I did was meet with the kids' new pediatrician. We had whittled a long list of specialists for the boys down to three—two for Anderson and one for Preston. At one time, that list had been in the teens. I felt grateful and I also couldn't help but feel the effects of the ongoing, of navigating life with a child with an intellectual disability. We experienced things with Anderson that we had not previously, things I will not write about.

I no longer grieved Anderson's diagnosis, and yet grief remained; it remains. There is a type of built-in grief that comes with loving someone more vulnerable. There is a grief that comes when you know the one you love will never be accepted by many, not fully. I was the happiest I had ever been & the ongoing grief I had always carried was heavier than I expected it to be.

———— *&* ————

It's only because we live on Florida's Space Coast that I found myself interviewing an astronaut one morning over coffee. Bob Cabana was a Marine before he put on a space suit. Once, he was rejected as a pilot due to a lack of visual acuity in his right eye, despite passing all his eye tests with 20/20 vision before and after that. After serving as an A-6 bombardier-navigator, he finally convinced military leaders to let him fly.

"At heart, I'm a pilot," he told me over his black cup of coffee.

Bob is older now; wrinkles greet the corner of his eyes, and thick salt-and-pepper hair covers his head. It was his experience as a twenty-something Naval Academy midshipman that set his big dream into motion. During a field trip to the Kennedy Space Center with the Physics Honor Society, he knew the direction he wanted his life to go—upward. After an initial rejection, Bob got accepted to the eleventh class of astronauts. He logged thirty-eight days in space, serving as a pilot and then mission commander. On his fourth flight, Bob made history as the first American to go to the International Space Station during its first assembly mission in 1998. He went on to become the director of the Kennedy Space Center before becoming the third highest ranking person at NASA, serving as the associate administrator leading eighteen thousand people before he retired in 2023.

I wanted to interview Bob not only because of his impressive career but also because I knew he had endured many hardships. Some are private, but another is public: He was the director of flight crew operations for the Columbia space shuttle mission in 2003. The astronauts never made it home. Bob knew each of those astronauts personally, and they were tremendous people, he said. Then, they were gone. Bob was the one to deliver the news to their families. I knew that my own perspective had changed and expanded after Disorder. I wanted to know how not only experiencing the unexpected but also having an out-of-this-world view had changed his.

At a sidewalk café on a breezy spring morning, he gave me a glimpse. He described what it was like, being a Minnesota boy, exiting the planet we all call home, and heading into space for the first time. He floated in silence, with only the hum of the cabin fans. Outside the windows, the Milky Way.

His galaxy, our galaxy, just one of billions, greeted him. The same stars he peered at as a boy on a northern Minnesota farm staring back at him still. And then he saw it—the curvature of Earth. Outside his window was a blue and green jewel. There was no division, only cohesion; it was the world as it should be—God's dream. Then, as he looked closer, he saw something else—a break. The Korean Peninsula was bright and shining from the south side, but darkness covered the land north of the DMZ, the demilitarized zone. It was almost as black as the space all around him. Almost. When he zoomed in, he saw the rainforest in Belize on fire. Then, smoke arising from burning oil fields—the cost of war.[1] Two hundred miles above Earth, he could see it so clearly—the chaos we create & the chaos we suffer.

There was something else too.

Over our planet, he saw a thin haze. That murky layer of protection is our atmosphere. It's all that separates us from the vacuum. As he stirred his coffee, Bob told me about the extreme conditions of outer space. On a spacewalk, astronauts can experience temperatures of 350 degrees Fahrenheit when the sun is out or negative 150 degrees on the sunless slide. When you are on the sunlit side of Earth, space is the absence of anything. "It's the blackest void you can imagine. Although there are stars there, you cannot see them. The sun is so bright that your irises close down so you only see the black void of space," Bob said. All that protects us from the void is this thin layer of protection.[2]

As I listened to Bob talk, I couldn't help but think, *This is what it means to be held.* In this life, we will know chaos. In this life, we will know what it means to have our heart broken. We will know broken people and broken leadership; we will know broken systems and the pain they inflict. We will know hurt on a planet where disease does not discriminate & we will be held in that hurt. Love does not eliminate chaos & yet holds us in it. Life is not compatible on any nearby planets and yet, on this blue and green jewel, we live. We are fragile & we live. We are not protected from it all & yet we are protected from nothingness. We live.

In 1929, astronomer Edwin Hubble and his associate Milton Humason made a groundbreaking discovery when measuring the redshift of spiral galaxies. The pair found that galaxies are moving away from Earth over time at upwards of hundreds of thousands of miles per second; the observation is now known as Hubble's Law.[3] Their discovery told us that the universe is still expanding. Astronomers call the mysterious force that is causing the cosmos to expand faster *dark energy*. However, scientists don't know why the universe still grows; they just know that each day the universe gets bigger and bigger.[4]

I am no scientist. I am just someone who thinks science and faith do not contradict but intertwine. I think God speaks to us in many ways. I think we are meant to keep learning. Learning about creation can lead us closer to the Creator. If God is love,[5] maybe the universe is still expanding because love cannot be contained. God's love pours out to the ends of the universe and does not stop. It's infinite. Love begets love. God's love is still creating, still imagining, still pushing against any limits we try to erect. God's love lets us choose & God's love holds us wherever we land. Love is the reason we are here & the reason we can endure. Love is why transformation through chaos is possible. Love is the reason there is a creation without end.

The Hubble Space Telescope was launched in 1990 and is the closest thing we have to a real-life time machine. Hubble works by gathering light from objects in our universe. That light takes time to reach the telescope, just as it takes time for light to travel from its source to our eyes. The sun is about 93 million miles from Earth. Sunlight takes eight minutes to reach us here on Earth. When we look toward the sun we are looking eight minutes into the past. Each picture Hubble captures shows what the object looked like years ago. In 2016, Hubble captured a groundbreaking discovery—a galaxy named GN-z11, observed as it was 13.4 billion years ago.[6]

We are so small & we have a God who loves us into significance. This God left the heavens and broke through to this one small planet in an infinite universe to live with us and for us. Jesus does not save us from all life's chaos. Jesus didn't save Himself from the worst the world has to offer. And yet, He holds the world together. He created life and makes life possible still. This life must be so very important. The God who created a vast universe billions of years ago, who expands the universe still, knows the number of hairs on our heads. It can only be love. What a gift. When life is what we imagined & when it is not—it is a miracle.

Bob described himself as a believer & a doubter. I looked at him and asked, "What if doubt is a portal to a deeper faith?" How could we not have questions upon questions living on one small planet in an incomprehensibly vast universe? I asked Bob if there was anything he was certain about, and his answer, as one who has witnessed up close the presence of other dimensions, did not surprise me: We will all die & death is not the end. "It's part of a process as we move forward. It's just a transition—it's a beginning to something better."[7] Being in the heavens confirmed that for him. Even when the worst came to pass, the terrible loss of his close friends and colleagues, he knew they were once again among the stars.

&

Hardships bring us closer to life. Something happens when living on the edge. The edge of before and after. The edge of life and death. Everything becomes more. The fog of busyness begins to dissipate when everything is teetering. Mundane leaves. Life sings a bit louder and it calls us to take notice. Our eyes catch the way the light bounces off the water. Our hearts take inventory of our views and how they need to be updated. We gain a heightened awareness of our pain and end up seeing others in theirs, maybe for the first time. Hardships bring us closer to the whole of life—the pain that is present & also the beauty. The chaos we know here on Earth can reveal what is important and what is not. An all-powerful Creator doesn't need hardships to be known & I have experienced how light often shines a bit brighter in our darkest times. This light points out things we might never have noticed before. We breathe in this good, difficult, ugly, & beautiful life and breathe out. We become more alive.

When we have been through those hard things that bring us to the edge, they also help us to see more clearly in our ongoing. It is why I wanted to capture every detail of those Friday mornings with Andy along the beach and sometimes still do. I wanted to soak in all of life's goodness because I realized what a gift it all was. Even if all is not right, so many things are. Going through Disorder gives us a glimpse of an out-of-this-world perspective. We know that life's chaos is never absent, not completely. & life's beauty is never completely absent either.

Life is too big to fit into the confines we place upon it. God is too big to fit into the boxes we create. I was starting to see that, yes, I would carry this grief of raising a child with an intellectual disability & that grief was directly tied to the love I had for him. We grieve because we love. There is no skipping to the good part. This is the good part: We love & that love can sometimes be so deep that it pains us. I thought love would erase the grief. Instead, grief & love coexist. Instead, love holds us in the chaos.

One morning on the beach, I was reminded of a conversation I had with a friend in Colorado who had a baby with Down syndrome. "Do you ever still wonder what he would be like if he didn't have Down syndrome?" she asked. Her question brought me back, back to when I was where she was. I remember feeling like the odd one out among family and friends. I was the twenty-something who had a child with a disability. I watched as their children hit the milestones at the appointed time on that dreaded chart, while mine wasn't even close. When they went to playdates, we went to therapy and preop appointments. My child was different, and so was I. Maybe this wasn't God's best for him, after all, I thought. Maybe this was just something that happened to him. And I would sometimes wonder what Down syndrome had taken away from him. And I would sometimes dream of who he would be without a disability. And I would sometimes wish that I could take that extra chromosome away.

Then time passed and my heart slowly changed as the calendar flipped from one year to the next. And I no longer wondered or dreamed or wished my child's disability away. Because I realized there is no Anderson without Down syndrome. There is no Anderson without his button nose or speckled eyes. There is no Anderson without his extra dose of intuition or empathetic touch. There is no Anderson without disability.

It doesn't mean I wouldn't lighten his load if I could. It doesn't mean that I don't still have some sad and tender feelings about his disability. But most, if not all, of those come from how the world sees him. Not how I see him.

I paused to answer my friend. I wanted to make sure I was telling her the truth. I realized that the truth was no. No, I never wonder, dream, or wish away my child's disability anymore. Maybe one day, she wouldn't either.

I realized what I told her in Colorado still held in Florida. It's just that I had to get used to living in the & alongside my child. When we are young, we do not dream of living life with pain. As we get older, we know pain is the cost of living & love is what makes living possible. The more we love, the more we have to lose. The more we love, the more we have to gain too. Love does not protect us from our vulnerability—it demands it. Love does not protect us from our fragility & it holds us in it.

Life after Disorder, life in the ongoing, is everything at once.

Life with my son is so difficult. Life with my son is so beautiful.

Life is so difficult. Life is so beautiful. All the time.

Life is not what I imagined when I was a teenager on Florida's beaches. Life will never quite be what I picture it to be because the picture is bigger than me. Standing on the beach as an adult, with the ongoing inside of me and fresh in a new beginning, I knew that I could only know so much. I stand in the harshness this universe contains & in the goodness it pours out. I stand in awe over how, all along, the God of the universe was making a way for us here.

When life is not as we imagined it, we can be grateful for a God who holds us in our losses and who creates something new and something good out of them. We can be thankful for a God whose love is still growing the universe and that this love can still grow in us.

After Disorder, the waters call us back. Can you hear their whispers? Step in and remember the One who first covered you. You do not need to be covered to become loved. You step into the water to remember that God says you already are. Right down to your fingertips. God chose you to be here in this still-expanding universe, chose you to live. The waters are calling you to the deep, to get more in touch with the God who lives within. This God who breathed you into being, who wants good things for you & who holds you in the chaos, wants to remind you that you were loved all those years ago. You will be loved until your dying day and beyond. Step into the water and know you will not always be shielded from Disorder or the heartache of the ongoing and know this: All of it can lead you to become more of who you already are, more of who you were created to be—God's dream.

FURTHER READING

Psalm 34

❖ REFLECTION ❖

How does the idea of being so small in the grand scheme of
the universe & so important land with you? Have you ever
felt disappointed that life wasn't perfect on the other side
of the unexpected, and how did you deal? God created life
to flourish; what does a flourishing look like for you now?

& GRATITUDE PRACTICE

I catch myself wanting to skip to the good part in this way:

I can see how the good part is already here in this way:

I feel small in this way:

I feel assured I am important when:

This is the ongoing grief/sadness I carry:

I can see how new life comes forth from it in this way:

12

Different & Grateful

I OPENED THE HEAVY CURTAINS of my hotel room and was greeted by my past. Shortly after my first book released, I got an email from a pastor and friend back in San Antonio asking me to deliver a Sunday morning sermon at his church. It would be our first time back in San Antonio since we left three years prior. It was an easy *yes*.

On an April morning, Andy and I rolled out of bed at 3 a.m. to make a red-eye flight from Florida to Texas. Thankfully, we got an early check-in at our hotel. I opened the curtains to our room to let the light in, as it was too early to take a nap. There it was—the San Antonio Children's Hospital in our direct line of sight.

I was in town to encourage people to undergo their suffering. Going all the way through Disorder doesn't mean we will find purpose behind it, and yet it is that process of digging into the deep, dark spaces, confronting the pain, sitting with that pain, and eventually pursuing healing that can lead us to new life. The scars of those who would hear me speak could be a catalyst for living into their God-dreamed entireties. Here I was, confronted by the place where so much of my past suffering unfolded. It was where Preston had been poked and prodded, it's where we and the ER doctor missed that his casts should have been replaced—resulting in a terrible injury that would scar him for life—it's where I feared he had taken his last breath when being admitted with RSV. It's where we spent many of our days, getting bloodwork done and trying to figure out his potassium levels once again. It's where we lived, and where we suffered. Now, here I was, about to tell the after story. I was living a new life because of the many deaths we had endured during our Disordered years.

We don't always get full-circle moments. Life often leaves us with question marks instead of exclamation points. Yet sometimes, God's grace brings us back to where life changed. My hand covered my mouth, as I tried to grasp my emotions. I looked at the rainbow-colored paneling on the building and knew: No, that time was not good & somehow, we survived. Somehow, we more than survived. Somehow, God wrangled goodness out of the harsh fluorescent-lit hallways where we once logged most of our hours, steps, and tears. I looked at my past & stood in my present and whispered, "Thank you."

I was not thankful for what kept us in that hospital. I was thankful for how God met me in those waiting rooms. I was thankful for the expansion of my heart that unfolded while sitting beside hospital beds. I was thankful for the resurrection not being just a story from thousands of years ago, but alive in my own. Once, I knew the thin line that separates this life and another. Because of Disorder, I experienced the death of many beliefs that shaped me and formed new ones.

Because of Disorder, I experienced a version of me that slowly slipped away and saw a different version emerge. Because of the Disorder, a new life began. Death and resurrection led me here—to this place where I would speak of the goodness that can come from life's inevitable pain. That goodness, most of the time, is a change from within.

Perhaps you will stand where you once stood and whisper, "Thank you." You may not find a cure in those words, but I hope you will experience healing.

&

They traveled together. They were all they had. Society had abandoned all ten of them. Their skin held signs of pain. Their pain was thought to be contagious. So, they were kept on the outside. They were forced out of their families and had to make a family out of each other. When they approached others, the law said they had to shout, "Unclean, unclean," so no one else would get close. Circles had been drawn around them, the boundaries not to be crossed. They were made to be their own jailers. They wore their ostracism on their skin and in their mouths. Segregation touched every aspect of their lives. They were cut off from the people they loved, cut off from the communities they knew, and cut off from experiencing God in the ways they had been taught.

Then, one day, they saw Him. They saw the man they had heard about, a man who had cured people just like them. They were desperate & they were hopeful. Instead of shouting, "Unclean!" as they had so many times before, a new song rolled off their tongues: "Jesus, Master, pity us!" He did. He sent them away to be observed by the priest as was customary to prove they were clean.[1] As they walked, their skin cleared. They were cured. Their sentences of being outsiders were revoked. The divide had been removed. They would no longer walk in chains but in freedom.

One man went back to Jesus. He could not contain his gratitude. He thanked Jesus, loudly, for all to hear. He was the only one. The others returned to their old lives. Not this man. He began something new. He was new. He was a Samaritan—an outsider by Jewish standards. Jesus looked at the grateful outsider and told him, "Your faith has made you well."[2]

In this story of the ten lepers found in Luke 17, all ten men were cured of their skin disease. All ten were cured of their social isolation. Only one man gave thanks. Nine men were cured physically; one, a Samaritan who had known isolation at a deeper level, being an outsider by Jewish standards, was healed. The Greek word used to tell the man he has been made whole, *sōzō*, can also mean *to be saved*.[3] This man was not only cured of his ailment, but he also experienced a deeper healing, a spiritual rescuing. Gratitude restores our souls to the Creator.

The outsider, who knew what it was like to be ostracized before his illness, had a heart of gratitude. The insiders missed it. They knew what Jesus could do, but they did not know who He was. Pain can help us understand life for what it really is—a gift. When we experience pain, we can let the hot sun dry up the goodness inside and become a shell of what we used to be. Or, we can let the crushing and the pressing make us softer than we once were. When we recognize life's goodness not as something we deserve but instead as a gift of grace, we become the opposite of hardened. Recognizing grace makes a way for grace to freely pour out of us.

The Greek noun *eucharistia* is used fifteen times in the New Testament and is usually translated as "thanksgiving." The verb *eucharisteō*, "to give thanks," occurs almost forty times. Jesus models gratitude—giving thanks to the source of life itself.[4] Gratitude must be so prevalent in Scripture because it's so important. In 1 Thessalonians 5:16–17, Paul writes, "Rejoice always, pray continually, give thanks in all circumstances; for this is God's will for you in Christ Jesus." We are not asked to give thanks *for* our circumstances. We are invited to give thanks *in* all circumstances. Giving thanks in all circumstances requires us to shift our thinking to this: Nothing belongs to us. Instead, every good thing is a gift.[5] Pain opens a door for us to become new. Gratitude is what takes our feet over the threshold. Gratitude does not cure us & gratitude can begin to heal us.

Because of pain & because of gratitude, the man who came back to thank Jesus would never be the same. The other nine men went back to their old lives when they were cured. But backward is not the direction we are meant to go. After Disorder hits, we are meant to walk forward to a new path because we are becoming something new. We are meant to evolve into our truest selves. The One who spoke the cosmos into existence, who loved us enough to let us choose, who loves us still, is always calling us home.

Jesus cured the men & it would take their own choices to experience a deeper healing. Gratitude is required for transformation. Gratitude opens up our souls for the healing work of the Divine to flow inward and then outward in our lives. Gratitude invites us to a resurrected way of living.

——— *&* ———

We attended many churches over our years living in various states. We have tried out cool churches with strobe lights, have sat in quiet, small churches with stained-glass windows, and have tried denominational and nondenominational congregations. Although all were very different, there is one thing they have in common—a big Easter Sunday celebration. We are all waiting for resurrection. We are all waiting for the good news: that death does not have the final say—love does. We sing hymns of gratitude, hallelujah pours from our lips, we have brunch, and then the next Sunday, a new sermon series starts. But we can't leave Easter in the rearview mirror. The resurrection is not just about what happened to Jesus after dying on the cross. The resurrection is alive in us. The love that resurrected Jesus is the same love that offers us new life again and again.

Because in this life, we will experience small deaths along the way. For me, it looked like years in and out of hospitals with my children; I still experience a sense of grief now and again alongside my child with an intellectual disability largely because of the societal barriers he faces. For you, the deaths might have been the physical death of someone you love, a betrayal, a loss of a relationship, a loss of community, or a chronic condition. Resurrection requires death, and death is painful. Resurrection is an awakening & it is more than that. Resurrection is about walking out of the graves that once held us & recognizing we can stand once more because of a strength that is not just our own. Resurrection is about where we go when we walk out of our graves. Resurrection is choosing to move forward with love after we have tasted death & experienced new life. Resurrection is choosing to live with eyes wide open to see the world we actually have—full of pain & full of beauty.

Death is required to become new & gratitude is required to live anew. Resurrection is not possible without gratitude. Without gratitude, we miss it. Because gratitude helps us to see that none of it belongs to us. Not the planet, not people, not even our worldly possessions. Instead, we get to be a part of it. We are a creation and we get to be a part of creation. We are loved and we get to love. We will know pain over and over again & there is no limit to experiencing resurrection. When we know life as a gift, we understand the source of life a little better, we understand ourselves better, and it changes how we live. Just as God still expands the universe, so does God call us into a deeper wholeness all of our days.

When we view the world through that lens—a lens that shows us we do not deserve anything and even so are given so much, our souls are restored to the One who dreamt us into being. None of it belongs to us; we all belong to the One who made us, the One who made it all. Even when life hands us something that is not a gift, if we undergo it in a way that we let it change us from the inside, that too can be a gift. Because God meets us in our pain, and if we are willing to participate in this meeting, we are not left the same. God still calls us to beauty. Beauty is found on the other side of pain & with the radical act of gratitude, beauty is even found *in* it.

———— & ————

A few months after coming full circle to San Antonio, we found ourselves vacationing in Grand Teton National Park—the site I opened this book with. The Tetons are unlike any mountain range I have ever seen. Unlike Pike's Peak, which greeted me every morning in Colorado with its relatively smooth dome, the Teton peaks are pointy and jagged. Their stark look is because of their age. Unlike the elderly Appalachian Mountains in the east, which are estimated to be around 300 million years old, and the middle-aged Rockies that are estimated to be somewhere around 50 to 80 million years old, the Tetons are one of the youngest mountain ranges in North America at only 10 million years old. Erosion has had less time to affect the Tetons, so the hard edges are largely intact.[6]

Andy and I had hiked for miles before sitting down to eat the protein bars we had packed. It was just the two of us, with our backs against a large tree trunk, staring at the Tetons. That's when he asked me the question.

"If you could go back and take it away—would you?" He was asking about the five years that upended life as we knew it, upended us as the people we once were. Would I go back and erase that part of our story if I could? I told him my truth: I would take back the pain my children experienced through Disorder if I could & if it were possible to separate my children's pain from my own, I would not take back my own.

Some events are just too tragic for this kind of answer, and then there are others. Other unexpected events that have had us teetering along the thin veil that separates this world from another, and we and the people we love somehow stayed on this side.

I think others who have brushed their fingertips along this veil may understand my answer. Because they know that perhaps they also wouldn't be who they are today without those long teary nights and endless close calls. We wouldn't be who we are today without the praying, the begging, the questioning, and the searching. We wouldn't be who we are today without our & stories.

My husband wasn't surprised. He agreed. When we get to this point, this point of not being grateful for everything that's happened to us but instead for the transformation that happened through the Disorder—that's Grace. Grace helps us move forward from bitterness to thankfulness, from defeat to peace, from pain to purpose, from grudge to forgiveness, from broken to transformed. Grace is what helps us to look back with pain in our hearts that lingers & also with gratitude in moving forward in the lives we now have as the changed people we've become.

We got up from our spot on the mountainside, and we walked hand in hand, knowing we would have been shocked by our answers only a year ago. We got up knowing that just because we are on the other side of hardship, that doesn't mean it won't come for us again. It was already there again, waiting for us at home with a child who didn't have physical pain but heart pain. We got up knowing that pain will always be near because life is painful & grace will carry us through again and again.

We were not like the young mountain range that stood before us. We had been touched by life. Our hard edges had been softened by pain & by grace. We had weathered years of Disorder and still stood. We had lived in this place of Reorder for nearly three years. For three years, we had been looking back and looking up. For three years we had stood in awe of what God had done in us. We were in awe of a God who said yes & who had said no. We were in awe of a God who allows bad things to enter our lives & who makes good and beautiful things in the aftermath. Sometimes life takes you to the edge of endings that end up beginning something new. Life as we knew it had ended & it began again.

We had walked the beach nearly every week for a year and thanked God for making us brave, for teaching us to dream, and for strengthening our love. We had thanked God for opening us to possibilities we had never thought possible. We thanked God for writing us home. Home not only in Florida but home to ourselves where God is so very present. We thanked God not for the heartache. We thanked God for how, through the heartache, we had become.

When we left the Tetons, we also left Reorder. We were entering a time of Order, a time that marks most of our lives, a time when life isn't marked by those life-changing unexpected moments nor big momentous milestones, a time when life is mostly a steady progression of small waves. A week after we got home, we walked on the beach once again. I looked at the ocean, standing in a black coverup, my natural curls tucked into a messy bun. I had Andy snap a picture of me. I had a song in my heart that needed to be sung. I went home and wrote. Some of these words would end up in a post for my online Facebook community:

Life can be good again. Only the good life is not like our old one, the one before the unexpected upended everything including us. The good life is not about getting our lives back, but instead, beginning life anew. Life may never be the same after experiencing the unexpected & yet it can be beautiful. It can be full of people. (Perhaps different people than you envisioned.) And it can be full of love.

God doesn't necessarily just take our broken pieces and put them back together. Oftentimes, God adds in new ones. The result is something different than what we started with. It has familiarity, yes. It has traces of what was. The darker shades remain in this sculpture & there are new vibrant hues too. God helps us to rebuild our lives while also rebuilding us in the process. The result is an ever-evolving, harsh, lovely, and good creation. It's a creation that is always expanding because that's what love does. Love is never done. We are never quite done. Thank God for that.

A good life is not necessarily an easier life. A good life comes when we are thankful for the life we have and the new person we are becoming. A good life is one we grow along with. A good life is one where we let Love transform us into who we were made to be. There can be a good life, a new life on the other side of Disorder when we return and say, "Thank you."

Once, I thought life was an equation to be solved. I thought there were many answers for me to find. Instead, I have found there to be many mysteries. One of the mysteries I find myself discovering again and again is that in this life, there will be death, & in this life there will be resurrection. God is in all things, including our stories. Especially in our resurrection stories. God is the grace that helps us to walk out of the graves that once held us and step into a different life. This different life may not be easier or better than the old & this different life can be full of love and purpose. This different life can be more fulfilling than we could ever have dreamed when inside our graves.

In and out and over again, the waves go out and the waves come in.

Sometimes we are pulled out by the waves & sometimes they gently bring us to the shore. When we get back to feeling the sand between our toes, we have a new understanding we gained while being tossed by the sea. We have known pain, and because of that pain, we are not who we once were. This newness leads us to live more gently & with a strength we did not know before the deep. We walk in the resurrected way now knowing:

Life is tragic & new life comes out of tragedies.

Life is ugly & beauty greets us every day.

Life is painful & healing is possible.

Life is maddening & sometimes the fire burns up what needs to die.

Life is confusing & grace meets us in the mystery.

Life brings us tears & those tears can help us to see things we once overlooked.

Life leaves us scarred & those scars can help us live into the fullest version of ourselves.

Life is full of small deaths & death is required to experience resurrection.

Life is full & a full life is everything at once.

Life is everything at once because we are fully alive.

Life is in the &.

Living in the & does not erase the painful past, nor the pain of the present.

Living in the & invites us to see life as it actually is—so hard & so good.

& is a new lens through which we see the world, ourselves, and the God who gives.

This God created all things out of love.

This Love is still expanding the universe & this Love is still expanding us.

& is a way to tap into this love because & is vulnerable.

& love requires vulnerability.

Love is why we are here & it is why there is always something to be grateful for.

God is transforming all things through love—including us.

Terrible things will happen here. Terrible things are happening here.

& Love has the final say in the grand universe and in our own lives.

With & we can be thankful for the life we have lived & the life we have right now.

Because all of it, the dark moments & light ones, brought us here.

We have known death & we live.

We have transformed & we are not done.

We are always becoming.

& this is a gift.

FURTHER READING

Psalm 30

❖ REFLECTION ❖

How can you envision resurrection playing out in your life now that you are living in the *&*? Viewing life through an *&* lens, how can your personal pain *&* gratitude help you live into your fullest self?

& GRATITUDE PRACTICE

Life is hard in this way:

Life is a gift in this way:

I am not thankful for:

I am thankful that it changed me in this way:

I have suffered death in this way:

I am living resurrection like this:

Acknowledgments

I'LL ADMIT, writing an acknowledgement section for a book with gratitude in the title is a bit overwhelming! (See what I did there.) In my first book, I thanked everyone I could think of who had brought me to this point—the point of becoming a published author.

This time, I want to thank those who shaped this message and brought it to life:

Andy, you will always be at the very top of my list of what I am grateful for.

Violet, you embody grace and have from such a young age, thank you. I hope to be more like you one day.

Anderson, you have given me a new lens through which I see the world and softer heart with which I experience it. I am so grateful.

Preston, your scars remind me of all we have been through & your humor reminds me how beautiful life always is.

To Mom and Dad, living near you both has enriched our lives tremendously and not just because of all the babysitting! Thank you for being a constant support to our overwhelm both in our past and in our present. Your presence marks our lives with joy, and I am so grateful.

To my sister Melissa, thank you for supporting my work and supporting me in every possible way. To both Melissa and my mother-in-law, Debbie, I am so grateful you both were witnesses to what went on in the sacred space that is the Ronald McDonald House. If there was a place that embodied the *&*, that was it. Thank you for experiencing it with me.

To my agent, Mary Demuth, who within minutes of my explaining the concept of this book knew exactly how to format it. You are such a talent and such a rare find in the publishing world with all you pour into your authors—thank you.

To my editor, Jennifer Dukes Lee, thank you for championing this book. There was no one else I wanted to publish with, and that's because of you. Let's do it again!

To my longtime mentor, Dan Brown, I was so lost at the beginning of this process. Thank you for lending me your ear, expertise, and guidance.

To the authors who have championed my work along the way: Leslie Means, Mikala Albertson, Amy Betters-Midtvedt, Jennifer Thompson, Jenny Albertson.

Perhaps the biggest thanks goes to my readers. This would not be possible without you. You kept me going. It was you who gave me the fuel to work on a wobbly table next to the burnt coffee station at the YMCA; it was you who kept me opening up my laptop while I had two kids in diapers and eighteen medical specialists between them. It's you who kept me writing. It was you who led me here. I am so grateful for every social media post you have shared and every email you have opened. Thank you, thank you, thank you. My greatest hope for you, for us, is that we can hold our real struggles in one hand *&* our real joys in the other at all times. My greatest hope for us is that we live fully—always.

Notes

Introduction

1. I am now told by family that this is not how the actual relative thought about where she lived. Even so, it speaks to the way many of us go through life. I've found myself at risk of this in my own life. The conversation that day was powerful enough to make a mark on me, changing the way I lived moving forward.

2. Tchiki Davis, "Toxic Positivity: Definition, Research & Examples," *The Berkeley Well-Being Institute*, accessed November 3, 2023, https://www.berkeleywellbeing.com /toxic-positivity.html.

3. Jainish Patel and Prittesh Patel, "Consequences of Repression of Emotion: Physical Health, Mental Health and General Well Being," *International Journal of Psychotherapy Practice and Research* 1, no. 3 (2019): 16–21, https://doi.org/10.14302/issn.2574-612X .ijpr-18-2564.

4. Benjamin P. Chapman et al., "Emotion Suppression and Mortality Risk Over a 12-Year Follow-up," *Journal of Psychosomatic Research*, 75, no. 4 (2013): 381, https://doi .org/10.1016/j.jpsychores.2013.07.014.

5. Brené Brown, *Braving the Wilderness: The Quest for True Belonging and the Courage to Stand Alone* (Random House, 2017), 67.

6. Harvard Health Publishing, "Giving Thanks Can Make You Happier," *Harvard Health*, August 14, 2021, www.health.harvard.edu/healthbeat/giving-thanks-can-make -you-happier.

7. Harvard Health, "Giving Thanks."

8. Misty Pratt, "The Science of Gratitude," *Mindful*, February 17, 2022, www.mindful .org/the-science-of-gratitude/.

9. Summer Allen, *The Science of Gratitude*, prepared for the John Templeton Foundation by the Greater Good Science Center at the University of California, Berkeley, May 2018.

10. Diana Butler Bass, *Grateful: The Transformative Power of Giving Thanks* (HarperCollins, 2018), 60.

11. "The History of 'Ampersand: How the '&' Got Its Name," *Merriam-Webster*, www .merriam-webster.com/grammar/the-history-of-ampersand.

12. Rachel Whalen (@unexpectedfamilyouting), "Five weeks after Dorothy died, my nephew was born," Facebook, December 26, 2018, https://www.facebook.com/photo/?fbid=2055818581171379&set=a.1470632053023371.

13. Walter Brueggemann, *Spirituality of the Psalms* (Augsburg Fortress, 2002), 8–9.

14. Brueggemann, *Spirituality of the Psalms*, 8.

15. Brueggemann, *Spirituality of the Psalms*, xiii.

16. Phillip Watkins quoted in Christina Caron, "Gratitude Really Is Good for You. Here's What the Science Shows," *New York Times*, June 8, 2023, www.nytimes.com/2023/06/08/well/mind/gratitude-health-benefits.html.

17. Caron, "Gratitude Really Is Good for You."

Chapter 1 Stressed & Grateful

1. "Stress in America 2014," Report Highlights, *American Psychological Association*, accessed June 12, 2024, www.apa.org/news/press/releases/stress/2014/highlights#:~:text=The%20most%20commonly%20reported%20sources.

2. "Stress," World Health Organization, February 21, 2023, https://www.who.int/news-room/questions-and-answers/item/stress.

3. "Upper Geyser Basin," Old Faithful Virtual Visitor Center, National Park Service, U.S. Department of the Interior, accessed June 12, 2024, www.nps.gov/features/yell/ofvec/exhibits/treasures/ugb/index.htm.

4. Brian McLaren, "Rewilding Christianity," BrianMcLaren.net, accessed December 10, 2023, http://brianmclaren.net/wp-content/uploads/2019/11/rewildingchristianity.pdf.

5. Richard Rohr, *The Universal Christ: How a Forgotten Reality Can Change Everything We See, Hope For, and Believe* (Convergent, 2019), 18.

6. Pete Enns, host, *Faith for Normal People*, podcast, "Episode 40: Anna Case-Winters—What Does It Mean for God to Be with Us?," June 10, 2024, thebiblefornormalpeople.com/episode-40-anna-case-winters-what-does-it-mean-for-god-to-be-with-us/.

7. Hope Reese, "How a Bit of Awe Can Improve Your Health," *New York Times*, January 3, 2023, www.nytimes.com/2023/01/03/well/live/awe-wonder-dacher-keltner.html.

8. Rangan Chatterjee, "The New Science of Awe & How It Improves Your Physical & Mental Wellbeing with Dr. Dacher Keltner," *Dr. Rangan Chatterjee*, March 1, 2023, drchatterjee.com/the-new-science-of-awe-how-it-improves-your-physical-mental-wellbeing-with-dr-dacher-keltner/.

9. Chatterjee, "The New Science of Awe."

10. Reese, "How a Bit of Awe Can Improve Your Health."

11. Reese, "How a Bit of Awe Can Improve Your Health."

12. Chatterjee, "The New Science of Awe."

13. Rohr, *The Universal Christ*, 16.

14. Reference to John 1.

15. Yang Bai et al., "Awe, the Diminished Self, and Collective Engagement: Universals and Cultural Variations in the Small Self," *Journal of Personality and Social Psychology* 113, no. 2 (2017): 185–209, https://doi.org/10.1037/pspa0000087.

16. Reese, "How a Bit of Awe Can Improve Your Health."

17. Ephesians 4:6.

Chapter 2 Longing & Grateful

1. Billie Bob Harrell Jr. as quoted in Steve McVicker, "Unlucky Strike," *Dallas Observer*, February 10, 2000, https://www.dallasobserver.com/news/unlucky-strike-6406997.

2. "Biggest Lottery Losers: Billie Bob Harrell Jr.," *Lotto Analyst*, accessed June 12, 2024, www.lottoanalyst.com/biggest-lottery-losers-billie-bob-harrell-jr.

3. Daniel Kahneman and Angus Deaton, "High Income Improves Evaluation of Life but Not Emotional Well-Being," *Proceedings of the National Academy of Sciences* 107, no. 38 (2010): 16489–93, https://doi.org/10.1073/pnas.1011492107.

4. J. Ehrlinger et al., "Decision-Making and Cognitive Biases," *Encyclopedia of Mental Health*, 2nd ed., Academic Press, January 1, 2016, www.sciencedirect.com/science/article/abs/pii/B9780123970459002068.

5. Jeremy Dean, "Impact Bias: Why We Overestimate Our Emotional Reactions," *PsyBlog*, June 16, 2021, www.spring.org.uk/2021/06/impact-bias.php.

6. Daniel Gilbert et al., "Immune Neglect: A Source of Durability Bias in Affective Forecasting," *Journal of Personality and Social Psychology* 75, no. 3 (1998): 617–38, https://doi.org/10.1037/0022-3514.75.3.617.

7. Daniel Gilbert on *The Happiness Lab with Dr. Laurie Santos*, podcast, "The Unhappy Millionaire," September 24, 2019, www.pushkin.fm/podcasts/the-happiness-lab-with-dr-laurie-santos/the-unhappy-millionaire.

8. Gilbert on *The Happiness Lab*.

9. Author's dramatic interpretation of John 4:1–42.

10. Miguel A. De La Torre, *Reading the Bible from the Margins* (Orbis, 2002), 125.

11. De La Torre, *Reading the Bible from the Margins*, 125.

12. Gail Wallace, "Revisiting the Woman at the Well in John 4, *The Junia Project*, March 15, 2021, https://juniaproject.com/revisiting-the-woman-at-the-well-in-john-4/.

13. Reference to John 3:16.

14. Reference to John 3:17.

15. Nathan Collins, "How Positive Thinking Can Backfire," *Greater Good*, February 5, 2016, greatergood.berkeley.edu/article/item/how_positive_thinking_can_backfire.

16. Summer Allen, "How Thinking About the Future Makes Life More Meaningful," *Greater Good*, May 1, 2019, greatergood.berkeley.edu/article/item/how_thinking_about_the_future_makes_life_more_meaningful.

17. Gabriele Oettingen et al., "Turning Fantasies about Positive and Negative Futures into Self-Improvement Goals." *Motivation and Emotion* 29, no. 4 (December 2005): 236–66, https://doi.org/10.1007/s11031-006-9016-y.

18. Gabriele Oettingen et al., "Mental Contrasting and Goal Commitment: The Mediating Role of Energization," *Personality and Social Psychology Bulletin* 35, no. 5 (2009): 608–22, https://doi.org/10.1177/0146167208330856.

19. Kelcey Grimes, "It's Not My Turn for Sleep or Romance, but It's My Turn to Soak Up the Magic of Raising Little Kids," *Her View from Home*, April 21, 2022, herviewfromhome.com/its-not-my-turn-for-sleep-or-romance-but-its-my-turn-to-soak-up-the-magic-of-raising-little-kids/.

Chapter 3 Busy & Grateful

1. Christopher K. Hsee et al., "Idleness Aversion and the Need for Justifiable Busyness," *Psychological Science* 21, no. 7 (July 2010): 926–30, https://doi.org/10.1177/0956797610374738.

2. Christine Carter, "Three Surprising Ways to Feel Less Busy," *Greater Good*, March 9, 2016, greatergood.berkeley.edu/article/item/3_surprising_ways_to_feel_less_busy.

3. Patrick van Kessel, "How Americans Feel About the Satisfactions and Stresses of Modern Life," *Pew Research Center*, February 5, 2020, www.pewresearch.org/short-reads/2020/02/05/how-americans-feel-about-the-satisfactions-and-stresses-of-modern-life/.

4. Exodus 18:14.

5. Exodus 18:17–18.

6. Reference to Galatians 6:2.

7. Andy Stanley, "Discovering God's Will 4," sermon, posted June 17, 2015, by Steve Roesch, YouTube, 7 min., 12 sec., www.youtube.com/watch?v=Dh9BCLdE_Vs.

8. Vanessa Patrick on Matt Abrahams, host, *Think Fast, Talk Smart*, podcast, episode 95, "The Power of No: How Boundaries Help Us Live More Empowered Lives," June 20, 2023, www.gsb.stanford.edu/insights/power-no-how-boundaries-help-us-live-more-empowered-lives.

9. "Book of Nehemiah Overview—Insight for Living Ministries," *Insight.org*, insight .org/resources/bible/the-historical-books/nehemiah#:~:text=Nehemiah%20recorded%20the%20reconstruction%20of.

10. Nehemiah 6:3 esv.

11. John 4:6 nlt.

12. Mark 6:30–32.

13. Luke 4:43.

14. David T. Neal et al., "Habits—A Repeat Performance," *Current Directions in Psychological Science*15, no. 4 (2006): 198–202, https://doi.org/10.1111/j.1467-8721.2006.00435.x.

15. Benjamin Gardner et al., "Making Health Habitual: The Psychology of 'Habit-Formation' and General Practice," *British Journal of General Practice* 62, no. 605 (2012): 664–66, www.ncbi.nlm.nih.gov/pmc/articles/PMC3505409/, https://doi.org/10.3399/bjgp12x659466.

16. Kristi DePaul, "What Does It Really Take to Build a New Habit?" *Harvard Business Review*, February 2, 2021, hbr.org/2021/02/what-does-it-really-take-to-build-a-new-habit.

17. Matthew 11:25; Luke 10:21; Matthew 15:36; Mark 8:6; John 6:11; 11:41; Luke 22:17, 19.

Chapter 4 Scared & Grateful

1. Rachel Nall, "How to Stop Catastrophizing," *Medical News Today*, November 30, 2023, https://www.medicalnewstoday.com/articles/320844.

2. Meg Jay, "What to Do When Your Mind (Always) Dwells on the Worst-Case Scenario," *Harvard Business Review*, September 15, 2020, hbr.org/2020/09/what-to-do-when-your-mind-always-dwells-on-the-worst-case-scenario.

3. Elizabeth R. Sowell et al., "In Vivo Evidence for Post-Adolescent Brain Maturation in Frontal and Striatal Regions," *Nature Neuroscience* 2, no. 10 (1999): 859–61, https://doi.org/10.1038/13154.

4. Nall, "How to Stop Catastrophizing."

5. Kendra Cherry, "Why Our Brains Are Hardwired to Focus on the Negative," *Verywell Mind*, November 13, 2023, www.verywellmind.com/negative-bias-4589618.

6. Cherry, "Why Our Brains Are Hardwired."

7. Amrisha Vaish et al., "Not All Emotions Are Created Equal: The Negativity Bias in Social-Emotional Development," *Psychological Bulletin* 134, no. 3 (2008): 383–403. https://doi.org/10.1037/0033-2909.134.3.383.

8. Tiffany A. Ito et al., "Negative Information Weighs More Heavily on the Brain: The Negativity Bias in Evaluative Categorizations," *Journal of Personality and Social Psychology* 75, no. 4 (1998): 887–900, https://doi:10.1037//0022-3514.75.4.887.

9. Reference to Matthew 6:34.

10. Kenneth S. Lane, "Tunnels and Underground Excavations," *Britannica*, updated April 27, 2023, www.britannica.com/technology/tunnel.

11. International Tunnelling and Underground Space Association, "Ancient Period," About Tunnelling, *ITA-AITES*, accessed June 24, 2024, tunnel.ita-aites.org/en/cases-his tories/history/ancient-period#:~:text=However%2C%20it%20seems%20that%20the.

12. Kelly Goldsmith et al., "Scarcity and Consumer Decision Making: Is Scarcity a Mindset, a Threat, a Reference Point, or a Journey?," *Journal of the Association for Consumer Research* 5, no. 4, (October 2020): 367–495, https://doi.org/10.1086/710531.

13. Emily Boynton, "4 Ways to Shed Scarcity Mindset and Increase Collaboration," *Right as Rain by UW Medicine*, October 4, 2022, rightasrain.uwmedicine.org/life/relationships/scarcity-mindset.

14. Boynton, "4 Ways to Shed Scarcity Mindset."

15. "Scarcity Mindset: Causes and How to Overcome It," *Cleveland Clinic*, November 20, 2022, health.clevelandclinic.org/scarcity-mindset.

16. Author's dramatic interpretation of the parable of the Rich Fool found in Luke 12:16–20.

17. Luke 12:13.

18. Luke 12:15.

19. William Barclay, *Daily Devotions with William Barclay: 365 Meditations on the Heart of the New Testament* (John Knox Press, 2008,) 327.

20. Luke Powery, "The Liturgy of Abundance: Luke 12:13–21," sermon, Duke University Chapel, August 4, 2013, https://chapel.duke.edu/sites/default/files/The%20Liturgy%20of%20Abundance%208-04-13.pdf.

21. Walter Brueggemann, "The Liturgy of Abundance, the Myth of Scarcity," *Religion Online*, accessed March 10, 2025, www.religion-online.org/article/the-liturgy-of-abundance-the-myth-of-scarcity/. The article originally appeared in *The Christian Century*, March 24–31, 1999.

22. Brueggemann, "The Liturgy of Abundance."

23. Wanchen Li et al., "Scarcity Mindset Reduces Empathic Responses to Others' Pain: The Behavioral and Neural Evidence," *Social Cognitive and Affective Neuroscience* 18, no. 1 (2023), https://doi.org/10.1093/scan/nsad012.

24. Boynton, "4 Ways to Shed Scarcity Mindset."

25. Brueggemann, "The Liturgy of Abundance."

26. John 10:10.

Chapter 5 Grieving & Grateful

1. "El Capitan Yosemite National Park," *Extranomical Tours*, accessed June 25, 2024, www.extranomical.com/el-capitan-yosemite-national-park/#:~:text=Geology.

2. "El Capitan," Extranomical Tours.

3. Oren Jay Sofer, "Gratitude and Grief—Ten Percent Happier," *Happier*, November 17, 2023, www.tenpercent.com/meditationweeklyblog/gratitude-and-grief.

4. Ann Finkbeiner, "The Biology of Grief," *New York Times*, April 22, 2021, www.nytimes.com/2021/04/22/well/what-happens-in-the-body-during-grief.html.

5. Francis Weller, "The Geography of Sorrow," *Science & Nonduality*, October 14, 2019, https://scienceandnonduality.com/article/the-geography-of-sorrow/.

6. Weller, "The Geography of Sorrow."

7. Weller, "The Geography of Sorrow."

8. Matthew 26:38.

9. Matthew 26:39.

10. Author's dramatic interpretation of Matthew 26:17–46.

11. Margaret Davis, "Physiological Process Behind Jesus' Crucifixion Revealed by Medical Experts," *Science Times*, April 2, 2023, www.sciencetimes.com/articles/43083/20230401/physiological-process-behind-crucifixion-jesus-christ-underwent.

12. Davis, "Physiological Process Behind Jesus' Crucifixion."

13. Davis, "Physiological Process Behind Jesus' Crucifixion."

14. Alok Jha, "How Did Crucifixion Kill?," *The Guardian*, April 8, 2004, www.theguardian.com/science/2004/apr/08/thisweekssciencequestions.

15. "Miscarriage," *Mayo Clinic*, September 8, 2023, www.mayoclinic.org/diseases-conditions/pregnancy-loss-miscarriage/symptoms-causes/syc-20354298.

16. "Gethsemane: Garden, Mount of Olives, Jerusalem," *Britannica*, accessed March 27, 2025, www.britannica.com/place/Gethsemane.

Chapter 6 Angry & Grateful

1. "Fighting Wildfires," *American Experience*, accessed March 13, 2025, www.pbs.org/wgbh/americanexperience/features/burn-fighting-wildfires/.

2. "Fighting Wildfires," *American Experience*.

3. Ben Jones, "How Do Wildfires Start?," *Dryad*, January 26, 2024, www.dryad.net/post/how-do-wildfires-start.

4. "The Ecological Benefits of Fire," Education, *National Geographic*, accessed March 13, 2015, education.nationalgeographic.org/resource/ecological-benefits-fire/.

5. "Wildfires," Encyclopedic Entry, *National Geographic*, accessed March 13, 2025, https://education.nationalgeographic.org/resource/wildfires/.

6. "Benefits of Fire," California Department of Forestry and Fire Protection, accessed February 25, 2025, https://www.fire.ca.gov/what-we-do/-/media/calfire-website/about/communications/benefitsoffire.pdf.

7. "The Ecological Benefits of Fire," *National Geographic*.

8. "Fighting Wildfires," *American Experience*.

9. Walter Brueggemann, *Spirituality of the Psalms* (Fortress Press, 2002), 38–39.

10. Albert R. Mohler, ed., New International Version Grace and Truth Study Bible (Zondervan, 2021), accessed April 8, 2025, via Bible Gateway, biblegateway.com/passage/?search=psalm%2013&version=NIV.

11. "Spire," *Friends of Notre Dame*, accessed March 14, 2025, https://www.friendsofnotredamedeparis.org/cathedral/artifacts/spire/.

12. Meg Matthias, "Notre-Dame Fire," July 30, 2024, *Britannica*, https://www.britannica.com/event/Notre-Dame-fire.

13. Agence France-Presse, "Notre Dame Rises from the Ashes: Macron Unveils Cathedral's Triumphant Comeback from 2019 Inferno," *Fortune*, November 29, 2024, https://fortune.com/europe/2024/11/29/notre-dame-rises-ashes-macron-unveils-cathedrals-triumphant-comeback-2019-inferno/.

14. Josh Hafner, "The Cross Still Stands and Votives Remained Lit. Signs of Hope out of the Notre Dame Cathedral Fire," *USA Today*, April 16, 2019, www.usatoday.com/story/news/world/2019/04/16/notre-dame-cathedral-fire-cross-still-standing-st-louis-tunic-hope/3482614002/.

15. Aurelien Breeden, "After Toppling in the 2019 Fire, Notre-Dame's Spire Rises Again," *New York Times*, December 8, 2023, www.nytimes.com/2023/12/08/world/europe/notre-dame-reopening-paris-france.html?auth=linked-google1tap.

16. Reference to Isaiah 61:3.

Chapter 7 Crying and Grateful

1. Mandy Oaklander, "The Science of Crying," *Time*, March 16, 2016, time.com /4254089/science-crying/.

2. Asmir Gracanin et al., "Why Crying Does and Sometimes Does Not Seem to Alleviate Mood: A Quasi-Experimental Study," *Motivation and Emotion* 39, no. 6 (2015): 953–60.

3. William H. Frey and Muriel Langseth, *Crying: The Mystery of Tears* (Winston Press, 1985), 45.

4. Frey and Langseth, *Crying: The Mystery of Tears*, 52–53.

5. Frey and Langseth, *Crying: The Mystery of Tears*, 55–57.

6. Benjamin Perry, *Cry, Baby: Why Our Tears Matter* (Broadleaf, 2023), 34.

7. Author's dramatic interpretation of John 20:1–12.

8. N. T. Wright on *Everything Happens with Kate Bowler*, podcast, season 11, episode 6, "N.T. Wright: The Mystery of God," October 10, 2023, https://katebowler.com/podcasts /the-mystery-of-god/.

9. John 20:17.

10. Clinton E. Arnold, ed., *Zondervan Illustrated Bible Backgrounds Commentary: New Testament* vol. 1 (2002), accessed April 1, 2025, via Bible Gateway, https://www.bible gateway.com/passage/?search=john%2020&version=NIV.

11. N. T. Wright, "The Easter Vocation," a sermon at the Eucharist in Durham Cathedral on Easter Morning 2006, *N.T. Wright Online*, accessed July 17, 2024, ntwrightpage .com/2016/03/30/the-easter-vocation/.

Chapter 8 Confused & Grateful

1. Ecclesiastes 1:2.

2. Pete Enns, host, *The Bible for Normal People*, podcast, episode 52: "Pete Enns—Ecclesiastes," June 11, 2018, thebiblefornormalpeople.com/ecclesiastes-with-pete-enns/.

3. Bill T. Arnold, *Introduction to the Old Testament (Introduction to Religion)* (Cambridge University Press, 2014), 376. Kindle.

4. Ecclesiastes 3:1–4.

5. Ecclesiastes 3:9–10.

6. Ecclesiastes 3:19.

7. John H. Walton, ed., *Zondervan Illustrated Bible Backgrounds Commentary: Old Testament* (2009), accessed April 1, 2025, via Bible Gateway, https://www.biblegateway.com /passage/?search=Ecclesiastes%203&version=NIV.

8. Ecclesiastes 12:13.

9. Enns, "Ecclesiastes," *The Bible for Normal People*.

Chapter 9 Scarred & Grateful

1. Wenke Shen et al., "Research Progress of Scar Repair and Its Influence on Physical and Mental Health," *International Journal of Burns and Trauma* 11, no. 6 (2021): 442–6, www.ncbi.nlm.nih.gov/pmc/articles/PMC8784744/.

2. Unnati Dusai, "Scars: A Guide to Good Healing," *Nuffield Health*, September 29, 2016, www.nuffieldhealth.com/article/scars-a-guide-to-good-healing#:~:text=After %20around%2021%20days%2C%20the.

3. Author's dramatic interpretation of Mark 8.

4. John Swinton, foreword to *Disability and the Way of Jesus: Holistic Healing in the Gospels and the Church*, by Bethany McKinny Fox (IVP Academic, 2019).

5. Clinton E. Arnold, ed., *Zondervan Illustrated Bible Backgrounds Commentary: New Testament* (2002), accessed April 1, 2025, via Bible Gateway, https://www.biblegateway.com/passage/?search=mark%208&version=NIV.

6. Walter Brueggemann, *Spirituality of the Psalms* (Facets, 2001), Kindle locations 473–5.

7. Reference to 2 Corinthians 12:9.

Chapter 10 Trust Looks Different Now & I'm Grateful

1. Author's dramatic interpretation of Matthew 21:1–11.

2. J. R. Daniel Kirk, "On Jesus' Choosing Twelve Men," *CBE International*, February 15, 2012, https://www.cbeinternational.org/resource/jesus-choosing-twelve-men/.

3. Mark 8:31–33.

4. Mark 9:30–32.

5. Mark 10:32–38.

6. Kirk, "On Jesus' Choosing Twelve Men."

7. Mark 14:8–9.

8. Reference to Matthew 5:3.

9. Tayor Fuerst, "Transformation Happens Here," sermon podcast, First United Methodist Church of Austin, November 26, 2023, *Apple Podcasts*, November 26, 2023, podcasts.apple.com/us/podcast/first-church/id276562947?i=1000636584772.

Chapter 11 Life Is Not What I Imagined & I'm Grateful

1. This section is from my interview with Bob Cabana on April 29, 2024, Bob's personal journal entry, and my own writings.

2. Interview with Bob Cabana.

3. Chelsea Gohd, "Dark Energy," *NASA*, updated March 7, 2024, science.nasa.gov/universe/the-universe-is-expanding-faster-these-days-and-dark-energy-is-responsible-so-what-is-dark-energy/.

4. Gohd, "Dark Energy."

5. 1 John 4:16 .

6. "Time Travel: Observing Cosmic History," *NASA*, updated February 26, 2025, science.nasa.gov/mission/hubble/science/science-behind-the-discoveries/time-travel-observing-cosmic-history/.

7. Interview with Bob Cabana.

Chapter 12 Different & Grateful

1. The Old Testament set out strict guidelines in Leviticus 13–14 for the examination and isolation of leprosy.

2. Author's dramatic interpretation of Luke 17:11–19.

3. Zondervan Illustrated Bible Dictionary Copyright © 1987, 2011 by Zondervan.

4. Matthew 11:25; 26:27; John 6:11; 11:41.

5. Referenced in James 1:17.

6. "Geologic Activity," Grand Teton National Park, Wyoming, *National Park Service*, updated May 14, 2024, www.nps.gov/grte/learn/nature/geology.htm.

JILLIAN BENFIELD

is a former journalist and news anchor and the author of *The Gift of the Unexpected: Discovering Who You Were Meant to Be When Life Goes Off Plan*. She holds a broadcast journalism degree from the University of Georgia. Her essays as a freelance writer have appeared on sites such as *TODAY*, *Good Morning America*, *Yahoo! News*, and *ABC News*. Jillian regularly advocates for the full inclusion of people with disabilities in her writings, in her community, and as a part of the National Down Syndrome Congress's National Down Syndrome Advocacy Coalition. Jillian and her husband, Andy, and their three children make their home on Florida's Space Coast. Learn more at JillianBenfield.com.

❖ CONNECT WITH JILLIAN ❖

JillianBenfield.com

⬤ @JillianBenfield

⬤ @JillianBenfieldBlog

www.ingramcontent.com/pod-product-compliance
Lightning Source LLC
Chambersburg PA
CBHW070030100426
42740CB00013B/2647